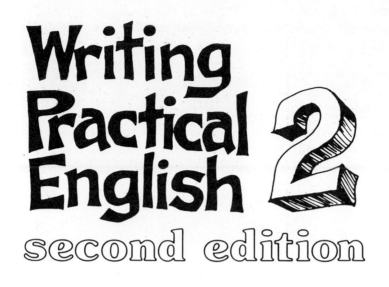

Writing Practical English 2

second edition

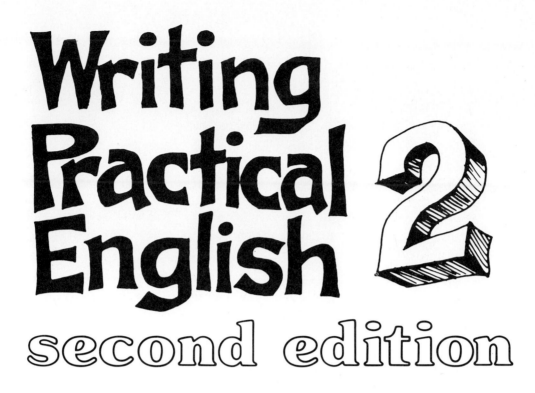

Writing Practical English 2

second edition

TIM HARRIS

Illustrated by **ALLAN ROWE**

HARCOURT BRACE JOVANOVICH, PUBLISHERS

SAN DIEGO   NEW YORK   CHICAGO   AUSTIN   WASHINGTON, D.C.
LONDON   SYDNEY   TOKYO   TORONTO

A NOTE TO THE INSTRUCTOR

The lessons in *Writing Practical English 2,* Second Edition, are closely coordinated with the lessons in the accompanying text, *Practical English 2,* Second Edition. They provide additional writing practice using the same grammatical items. Exercises from this workbook should be assigned only after the corresponding material in the text has been covered in class. A few vocabulary items are used here before they appear in the text, but the meanings of these words are always made clear by the accompanying illustrations.

It is generally a good idea for instructors to go over the workbook exercises orally in class before assigning them as homework. This applies particularly to the picture compositions. Instructors should have students discuss a given picture in class before asking them to write a composition about it. Instructors should also explain any unfamiliar vocabulary that the students will need to know in writing their compositions.

CONTENTS

1

CHAPTER ONE

A lot/much/many   A little/a few

a *Look at the pictures and write a negative sentence for each one using* **much** *and* **many.**

1. salad / bowl

There isn't much salad in the bowl.

2. leaves / tree

There aren't many leaves on the tree.

3. flowers / vase

4. orange juice / bottle

5. glasses / shelf

6. books / bookcase

7. gas / tank

8. cars / parking lot

4

MUCH

| They don't need | much | paper. |

ONLY A LITTLE

| They need | only a little | paper. |

MANY

| She didn't take | many | envelopes. |

ONLY A FEW

| She took | only a few | envelopes. |

b *Change the following sentences using **only a little** and **only a few**.*

Examples: They don't have much money.

They have only a little money.

She didn't know many people in New York.

She knew only a few people in New York.

1. They don't have many friends.

   _____

2. He doesn't put much sugar in his coffee.

   _____

3. She doesn't want much ice cream for dessert.

   _____

4. We didn't go to many parties last year.

   _____

5. He didn't sell many books last week.

   _____

6. They didn't have much free time last month.

   _____

7. She doesn't get many letters.

   _____

8. He doesn't speak much Italian.

   _____

9. They don't understand many words in French.

   _____

HOW MUCH and HOW MANY

How much sugar	do they have?
How many oranges	

c *Make questions with **how much** and **how many**.*

Examples: shampoo *How much shampoo do you need?* _____

matches *How many matches do you need?* _____

1. paper _____

2. envelopes _____

3. stamps _____

4. soap _____

5. toothpaste _____

6. glasses _____

7. sugar _____

8. eggs _____

9. butter _____

d *Write five sentences using **a lot of**.*

Examples: *I have a lot of magazines at home.*

There's a lot of milk in the refrigerator.

1. _____

2. _____

3. _____

4. _____

5. _____

Tino and his friends are having a picnic.

Tino (hot dogs)   Johnnie (glasses)   Barbara (skirt)
Barney (cap)   Gloria (coffee pot)   Peter (cards)
Dr. Pasto (beard)   Otis (binoculars)   Maria (cards)

e *Write sentences that describe what each of them is doing, using the present continuous.*

Examples: Tino is cooking hot dogs.   Barney is eating.

f *Write sentences about the objects in the pictures on pages 6 and 7 using a lot of, a few, and a little.*

Examples:

wood/next to the fireplace *There's a lot of wood next to the fireplace.*

hot dogs/on the grill *There are a few hot dogs on the grill.*

ketchup/in the bottle *There's a little ketchup in the bottle.*

1. lemonade/in the pitcher _____

2. ice cream/in the carton _____

3. flowers/in the vase _____

4. mustard/in the jar _____

5. coffee/in the pot _____

6. people/at the picnic _____

7. bicycles/under the tree _____

8. birds/in the tree _____

8

g *Write a short composition about the pictures on pages 6 and 7. Use the present continuous, **there is**, and **there are**.*

cook	have	point to	sit
eat	look at	pour	stand
drink	play	shine	talk

PRONUNCIATION

h *List the following words in the blanks below according to the underlined vowel sound.*

student	fruit	club	summer
lunch	soup	include	stupid
husband	couple	uncle	young
true	blue	truck	study
number	boot	Tuesday	juice

truth

student _____

bus

lunch _____

_____ _____ _____ _____

_____ _____ _____ _____

_____ _____ _____ _____

_____ _____ _____ _____

i *Underline the stressed vowel sounds.*

Example: personality

company	disappear	appetite	lemonade
understand	conversation	however	customer
passenger	telephone	shampoo	emergency
energetic	refrigerator	motorcycle	afternoon
unfortunately	interesting	intelligent	representative
original	expensive	library	radiator

j *Complete the following sentences using the simple present or the present continuous.*

Examples: Mabel (go) _____*goes*_____ to the market every day.

Look! Some boys (play) *are playing* football in the street.

1. Anne (leave) _____ the office now.

2. She usually (take) _____ the bus home.

3. Listen! Someone (call) _____ you.

4. It's Marty. He (come) _____ here every day.

5. Please be quiet. I (do) _____ my homework.

6. Linda (go) _____ to a movie with Albert tonight.

7. They often (go) _____ to the movies together.

8. We (play) _____ tennis with them twice a week.

9. Look! Maria (wear) _____ her new dress.

10. She always (wear) _____ nice clothes.

11. The post office (close) _____ at 12 o'clock on Saturdays.

12. Sam is busy now. He (clean) _____ the garage.

k *Complete the following sentences with suitable prepositions.*

Example: I looked *out* the window and saw a dog *in* the garden.

1. Barbara lives _____ the house across the street _____ the library.

2. She usually takes the bus _____ work _____ the morning.

3. She works _____ nine _____ five.

4. She likes to read _____ the evening when she comes home _____ work.

5. I like to watch TV _____ my friends.

6. I can't see the TV when you stand _____ it.

7. Why don't you sit _____ the sofa?

8. My favorite program starts _____ five o'clock.

9. It's the movie _____ the week.

10

l *Complete the following sentences using subject pronouns and object pronouns.*

Examples: Gloria is lucky. _____*She*_____ has a good job.

I'm not ready. Please wait for _____*me*_____ .

1. Where are the boys? Are _____ at the park?

2. Sam knows the answer. Ask _____ .

3. We're having a problem. Can you help _____ ?

4. Don't ask me for money. _____ don't have any.

5. Peter's car is in good condition. _____ takes good care of _____ .

6. Let's go to a movie. _____ can see *Star Wars* at the Odeon.

7. Who is that woman? Do you know _____ ?

8. Her name is Barbara. _____ works at the City Bank.

9. Mmm, these cookies are delicious. Did you make _____ ?

10. Please give me your telephone number so _____ can call _____ .

m *Complete the following sentences using **can't** + an appropriate verb.*

Examples: Ed is lazy. He *can't get up* in the morning.

I don't have a pen. I *can't write* a letter.

1. It's raining. We _____ tennis today.

2. There's a car coming. You _____ the street.

3. Anne doesn't have the key. She _____ the door.

4. It's dark in this room. We _____ our books.

5. Where are Jimmy's socks? He _____ them.

6. This coffee is too hot. I _____ it.

7. The girls have to do their homework. They _____ to the movies.

8. Tony doesn't have Jane's phone number. He _____ her.

9. That sofa is too expensive. We _____ it.

10. Those people are talking in a foreign language. I _____ them.

CHAPTER TWO

Like to/want to/ have to

Present continuous for future

a   *What do they like to do?*

1. *She likes to talk on the telephone.*

2. *They like to read.*

3.

4.

5.

6.

7.

8.

14

1. *They want to rest.*

2. *He wants to sell more books.*

3.

4.

5.

6.

7.

8.

c   *Make questions with who, what, where, or when.*

Examples: He wants to play tennis <u>in the park</u>.

Where does he want to play tennis?

She wants to talk to <u>her mother</u>.

Who does she want to talk to?

They want to buy <u>a car</u>.

What do they want to buy?

They want to travel <u>next month</u>.

When do they want to travel?

1.   He wants to call <u>his girlfriend</u>.

_____

2.   She wants to live <u>in Montreal</u>.

_____

3.   They want to know <u>your address</u>.

_____

4.   They want to see the paintings <u>tomorrow</u>.

_____

5.   My brother wants to go <u>to the movies</u>.

_____

6.   He wants to leave <u>at ten o'clock</u>.

_____

7.   Barney wants to have lunch with <u>Nancy</u>.

_____

8.   He wants to meet her <u>at noon</u>.

_____

9.   He wants to take her <u>to Joe's Cafe</u>.

_____

10.   He wants to have <u>a hamburger</u> for lunch.

_____

d *Look at the pictures and answer the questions using* **have to**.

1. Why can't Mabel talk on the phone now?

   She has to make dinner.

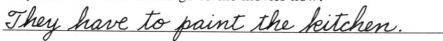

2. Why can't Otis and Gloria go to the movies now?

   They have to paint the kitchen.

3. Why can't Marty watch television now?

4. Why can't Anne and Barbara go to lunch now?

5. Why can't Jimmy and Linda see their friends now?

6. Why can't Tino play tennis now?

7. Why can't Sam and Mabel go to the park now?

8. Why can't Johnnie read the newspaper now?

e *List five things you like to do in your free time.*

Example: *I like to play tennis.* _____

1. _____
2. _____
3. _____
4. _____
5. _____

f *List five things you want to do this month or this year.*

Example: *I want to find an interesting job.* _____

1. _____
2. _____
3. _____
4. _____
5. _____

g *List five things you have to do every day or every week.*

Example: *I have to get up early in the morning.* _____

1. _____
2. _____
3. _____
4. _____
5. _____

18

h *Complete the following sentences using the word **but**.*

Examples: Paris is a beautiful city, *but it's very expensive.*

We like to travel, *but we don't have much money.*

1. I studied French for six months, _____

2. The Rose Cafe has good food, _____

3. Anne works hard, _____

4. She's a nice person, _____

5. Mr. Poole is very intelligent, _____

6. He has an old car, _____

7. His wife isn't very pretty, _____

8. They don't have much money, _____

9. Their apartment is small, _____

i *Complete the following sentences using the word **so**.*

Examples: Jack's car was dirty, *so he washed it.*

Mrs. Hamby wants to lose weight, *so she eats very little.*

1. The weather wasn't very good yesterday, _____

2. Barney needed some money, _____

3. Ula Hackey has a lot of money, _____

4. I don't have a car, _____

5. We were tired, _____

6. Barbara liked the dress and it was on sale, _____

7. The party at the Disco Club wasn't very good, _____

8. I was hungry, _____

9. Mr. Bascomb was in a hurry, _____

j *Answer the questions about the pictures with an affirmative sentence and a negative sentence, as indicated.*

1. Did Peter go out with Maria or Sandy last night?

   He went out with Maria.
   He didn't go out with Sandy.

2. Did he bring her chocolates or flowers?

   _____

   _____

3. Did Maria wear a white dress or a black dress?

   _____

   _____

4. Did they go in Maria's car or Peter's car?

   _____

   _____

5. Did they eat in a Chinese restaurant or a French restaurant?

_____

_____

6. Did they sit next to a window or in the corner?

_____

_____

7. Did they have chicken or fish for dinner?

_____

_____

8. Did they drink red wine or white wine?

_____

_____

k *Write a short composition about Maria's date with Peter. Add some details. How did Peter and Maria dress? What was the restaurant like? How was the food? Was it a special evening or just an ordinary date?*

CHAPTER THREE

Both/neither/all/none
"Which (one) . . . ?"

Some/any compounds
Must (logical conclusion)

a *Look at the pictures and write two sentences for each one using **all**, **none**, **both**, or **neither**.*

USED BICYCLES
$19⁰⁰ $23⁰⁰

1. bicycles / cheap / expensive

Both of these bicycles are cheap.
Neither of them is expensive.

2. girls / thin / fat

None of these girls are thin.
All of them are fat.

3. cars / new / old

_____
_____

4. boys / tall / short

_____
_____

5. apples / good / bad

_____
_____

6. men / strong / weak

_____
_____

7. pots / clean / dirty

_____
_____

8. women / young / old

_____
_____

Compounds of SOME and ANY   Affirmative

They're	talking to	someone.
	buying	something.
	going	somewhere.

Negative

They aren't	talking to	anyone.
	buying	anything.
	going	anywhere.

b   *Complete the following sentences using* **some, someone, something, somewhere, any, anyone, anything,** *and* **anywhere.**

Examples: Sam doesn't have ___*any*___ friends in Los Angeles.

Does he know ___*anyone*___ in San Francisco?

Yes, he met ___*someone*___ from San Francisco last week.

1. Mrs. Golo didn't buy _____ at the market today.

2. Did she buy _____ yesterday?

3. Yes, she got _____ for the cat.

4. Where's my pen? I can't find it _____ .

5. It's probably _____ in the living room.

6. There are _____ people here to see Mr. Golo.

7. He's sick. He can't see _____ today.

8. I'm hungry. Let's go _____ for lunch.

9. Good idea. But let's not go _____ expensive.

10. _____ told me there's a good cheap restaurant on Clark Street. I think it was Peter Smith.

11. Peter and Maria are at the restaurant now. Peter is saying _____ to the waiter, but the waiter can't hear _____ because of the noise.

12. Barbara didn't write to _____ last night.

13. She didn't have _____ free time.

14. Mr. Bascomb had an important meeting yesterday with _____ from New York.

c *Find the opposites and fill in the banks.*

cold	far	winter
future	last	a little
slowly	none	low
poor	stupid	sad
start	arrive	loan
dirty	cloudy	answer

1. stop *start*

2. all _____

3. happy _____

4. past _____

5. near _____

6. sunny _____

7. high _____

8. quickly _____

9. borrow _____

10. clean _____

11. a lot _____

12. leave _____

13. first _____

14. summer _____

15. hot _____

16. ask _____

17. rich _____

18. intelligent _____

d *Complete the following sentences using a lot of, much, many, a few, and a little.*

Examples: When Maria washes her hair she uses only *a little* shampoo.

How *much* shampoo do you use?

1. Everyone likes Sam. He has _____ friends.

2. He works hard, but he doesn't make _____ money.

3. Jack is lazy. He works only _____ hours a day.

4. How _____ hours do you work?

5. I don't do _____ work, but I have _____ fun.

6. Linda is going to be a good dancer. She just needs _____ practice.

7. Unfortunately, she only has time to dance _____ hours a week.

8. She's really something. You don't see _____ girls like her.

9. We went to a big party at the Country Club. There were _____ people there.

10. I wasn't hungry, so I didn't eat _____ . I just had _____ cake.

e   *Look at the pictures and write a sentence for each one using* **must**.

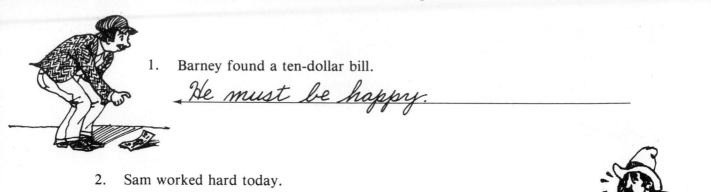

1.   Barney found a ten-dollar bill.

He must be happy.

2.   Sam worked hard today.

_____

3.   Jack doesn't like to work.

◄_____

4.   Anne takes three showers a day.

_____►

5.   Albert is having four hamburgers for lunch.

◄_____

6.   Tino can lift almost anything.

_____►

7.   Ula Hackey wears very expensive clothes.

◄_____

8.   Dr. Pasto can discuss anything.

_____►

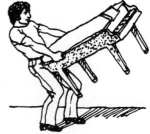

f   *Complete the following sentences using the word **because**.*

Examples: She walks to work *because she doesn't have a car.*

I'm taking my umbrella *because it's raining.*

1.   I'm happy _____

2.   We eat at Joe's Cafe _____

3.   People like Sam _____

4.   He didn't go to work yesterday _____

5.   Gloria is tired _____

6.   She sold her car _____

g   *Complete the following sentences.*

Examples: Although he's a good tennis player, *he doesn't win many games.*

Although it wasn't very late, *we went home.*

1.   Although she's rich, _____

2.   Although she lived in France for two years, _____

3.   Although the weather was good yesterday, _____

4.   Although I wasn't very tired, _____

5.   Although he's busy, _____

6.   Although he works hard, _____

h   *Make questions with the words given below.*

Examples: why *Why is she always late?*

which *Which book is yours?*

1.   when _____

2.   where _____

3.   why _____

4.   what _____

5.   which _____

6.   whose _____

28

i   Complete each of the following sentences with an appropriate verb. Use the simple present tense or the present continuous.

Examples: Jimmy is in the bathroom. He _is brushing_ his teeth.

He _brushes_ his teeth after every meal.

1. Mrs. Golo _____ the newspaper every morning.

   Her husband is in the living room. He _____ a book.

2. Sam can't come to the phone because he _____ a shower.

   He _____ a shower twice a day.

3. Albert usually _____ at the library.

   The library is closed today, so Albert _____ at home.

4. Nancy is busy now. She _____ a letter to her family.

   She _____ them a letter every week.

5. Mr. Bascomb is in the kitchen. He _____ a cup of coffee.

   His wife never _____ coffee. She doesn't like it.

6. Otis is a good artist. He _____ beautiful pictures.

   Today he _____ a picture of the ocean.

7. Look at Barbara. She _____ a beautiful dress.

   She always _____ nice clothes.

8. It's five-thirty. I _____ home now.

   I _____ home at five-thirty every day.

9. Take your umbrella. It _____ .

   It always _____ in March.

10. Johnnie complains every time Ed _____ his cigar in the living room.

    Johnnie is angry because Ed _____ a big cigar right now.

FALL SALE 5 days only Oct. 8-12.

Save 50% and more on Quality Menswear.

Sport Coats
Regular price $150
Sale Price $70⁰⁰

Dress Shirts
Regular Price $35
Sale Price $15⁰⁰

Wool Slacks
Regular price $90
Sale Price $45⁰⁰

• HOURS: Monday thru Saturday 9 a.m. – 6 p.m. ★ Closed Sundays ★

CONTINENTAL MEN'S SHOP since 1938

835 Main Street (½ block east of Lime St.)

j *Answer the following questions about the advertisement.*

1. When does the sale start? *It starts October 8th.* _____

2. How long does the sale last? _____

3. What is the regular price of sport coats? _____

4. What is the sale price of sport coats? _____

5. How much can you save on sport coats during the sale? _____

6. How much can you save on dress shirts? _____

7. How much can you save on wool slacks? _____

8. What hours is the store open? _____

9. Is the store open on Sundays? _____

10. What's the address of the Continental Men's Shop? _____

30

k *Complete the following sentences using **going to** + verb. Make affirmative sentences.*

Examples: Jack is broke. He *'s going to borrow* some money from Sam.

Don't worry. We *'re going to be* on time for the meeting.

1. It's hot in here. I _____ the window.

2. We don't like the color of the kitchen. We _____ it a different color.

3. Mabel is taking some food from the refrigerator. She _____ lunch.

4. Sam is looking for the toothpaste. He _____ his teeth.

5. Linda is walking to the stationery store. She _____ some paper.

6. Bob likes Linda. He _____ her for a date.

l *Complete the following sentences using **going to** + verb. Make negative sentences.*

Examples: They need their car. They *aren't going to sell* it.

Jimmy has a headache. He *isn't going to do* his homework tonight.

1. Mr. Bascomb is in a hurry. He _____ breakfast this morning.

2. Leave your umbrella at home. It _____ .

3. Sandy likes to wear her hair long. She _____ it.

4. I don't like Tony. I _____ him to my party.

5. Mabel _____ dinner tonight. She's going to a restaurant.

6. That table is too expensive. We _____ it.

m *Change from singular to plural.*

1. foot *feet*
2. shoe *shoes*
3. box _____
4. glass _____
5. dish _____
6. knife _____

7. fork _____
8. lunch _____
9. party _____
10. game _____
11. child _____
12. tooth _____

13. brush _____
14. leaf _____
15. tree _____
16. church _____
17. hobby _____
18. toy _____

CHAPTER FOUR

Review

a *Write sentences about the two men in the picture using **one**, **both**, or **neither**.*

Examples: old *Both of them are old.*

young *Neither of them is young.*

watch *One of them is wearing a watch.*

1. coat _____

2. tie _____

3. T-shirt _____

4. hats _____

5. socks _____

6. tennis shoes _____

7. short _____

8. rich _____

9. lazy _____

10. thin _____

11. happy _____

12. sad _____

34

b *Choose an adverb of frequency and write a true sentence about yourself.*

Example: cook dinner *I often cook dinner.*

OR *I hardly ever cook dinner.*

1. take the bus _____

2. drink coffee _____

3. read comic books _____

4. listen to classical music _____

5. go to parties _____

6. wear tennis shoes _____

7. play cards _____

8. fall asleep in class _____

9. try to help people _____

10. tell the truth _____

c *Complete the following sentences.*

Example: We don't often *go to the movies.*

1. Last night _____

2. What kind _____

3. Please don't _____

4. They never _____

5. When she got home, _____

6. Do you think _____

7. He's worried because _____

8. I don't like it when _____

9. How often _____

10. When are you going to _____

11. Well, to be honest, _____

12. It takes me a long time to _____

d *Write sentences about the women in the picture using* **some, all,** *or* **none.**

Examples: healthy *All of them are healthy.*

sick *None of them are sick.*

tennis shoes *Some of them are wearing tennis shoes.*

1. old _____

2. short _____

3. hats _____

4. coats _____

5. neat _____

6. fat _____

7. watches _____

8. glasses _____

9. pretty _____

10. tall _____

11. jeans _____

12. dresses _____

36

e *Rewrite the following sentences using the adverbs indicated.*

Examples: (now) Are they working? *Are they working now?*

(still) Yes, they're at the office. *Yes, they're still at the office.*

(perhaps) We can see them later. *Perhaps we can see them later.*

1. (here) Ula Hackey is in town! _____

2. (twice) I called her at the hotel. _____

3. (unfortunately) She wasn't available. _____

4. (very) They said she was tired. _____

5. (early) She went to bed. _____

6. (maybe) We can see her tomorrow. _____

7. (really) I like Miss Hackey. _____

8. (always) She makes good movies. _____

9. (terribly) She's romantic. _____

10. (again) Let's call her in the morning. _____

11. (somewhere) Perhaps we can meet her. _____

12. (then) We can get her autograph. _____

f *Write original sentences using the adverbs given below.*

Example: there *The keys are there on the table.*

1. really _____

2. again _____

3. maybe _____

4. now _____

5. very _____

6. unfortunately _____

7. anywhere _____

8. twice _____

9. still _____

INDEFINITE ARTICLES

We use **a/an** before a singular countable noun, **a** before a consonant sound: **a** car, **a** girl and **an** before a vowel sound: **an** apple, **an** umbrella

Use **a/an**:

1. to talk about a class of people or things.
   He's **a** doctor.   We need **a** car.

2. to talk about a person or thing for the first time.
   I received **a** letter yesterday.   The letter was from my sister in New York.
   A man is talking to **a** woman.   The man is short and the woman is tall.

3. for a person or thing that we can't (or don't want to) identify specifically.
   A man phoned this morning.   The police are looking for **a** woman in a green car.

4. when you mean ''one.''
   I'm going home in **an** hour.   Can you loan me **a** dollar?

Do not use **a/an**:

1. before plural nouns.
   She bought some magazines.   NOT: She bought a magazines.

2. before uncountable nouns (including abstract nouns like freedom and happiness).
   They don't eat meat.   NOT: They don't eat a meat.

---

g   *Insert **a** or **an** if necessary.*

Examples: I'm having *a* problem with one of my neighbors.

Do you ever have _____ problems with your neighbors?

1. Barbara is _____ good secretary.

   _____ good secretaries are hard to find.

2. Peter seldom makes _____ mistakes.

   But he made _____ big mistake yesterday.

3. French is _____ important language.

   Can you speak _____ French?

4. They sell _____ bread at the market.

   I'm going to buy _____ loaf of bread.

5. _____ milk is good for you.

   Do you want _____ glass of milk?

6. I eat _____ beans because they're cheap.

   _____ can of beans costs only thirty cents.

7. Do you like _____ hamburgers?

   I had _____ hamburger for lunch today.

8. Look! There's _____ fly in your soup.

   Oh, no. I hate _____ flies.

9. My favorite dessert is _____ ice cream

   I want _____ ice cream cone for dessert.

10. Peter gave Maria _____ red rose.

    Maria loves _____ roses.

11. Do you like _____ tea?

    There's _____ pot of tea on the stove.

12. What _____ beautiful day!

    I love _____ days like this.

DEFINITE ARTICLE

We use **the** to identify specific people or things. **The** is used with countable nouns: **the** table, **the** books   and with uncountable nouns: **the** rain, **the** weather

Use **the**:

1. the second time you talk about a person or thing.
   I received a letter yesterday. **The** letter was from my sister in New York.
   A man is talking to a woman. **The** man is short and **the** woman is tall.

2. when the situation makes it clear which people or things you are talking about.
   Please close **the** door.   ''Where's **the** milk?''   ''I drank it.''

3. when the phrase used after the noun makes the noun specific.
   I like **the** music of Brazil.   **The** book she bought is on the desk.

4. before rivers, seas or oceans, groups of islands, chains of mountains, and with some countries.
   The Hawaiian Islands are in **the** Pacific Ocean.
   The Mississippi River is in **the** United States.

Do not use **the**:

1. to talk about things in general.
   Milk is good for you.   NOT: The milk is good for you.
   Books are expensive.   NOT: The books are expensive.

2. with streets, roads, countries or continents.
   France is in Europe.   NOT: The France is in the Europe.
   They live on Bond St.   NOT: They live on the Bond St.

---

h *Insert **the** if necessary.*

Examples: I like to meet _____ people.

Who are *the* people over there?

1. You need _____ flour to make bread.

   Where did you put _____ flour?

2. _____ weather today is very warm.

   Do you like _____ warm weather?

3. Most students have _____ dictionaries.

   _____ dictionary on the table is Jane's.

4. I like to read _____ magazines.

   Can I read _____ magazines on your desk?

5. _____ air in this city is clean.

   It's important to have clean _____ air.

6. Anne usually goes to work by _____ bus.

   She takes _____ same bus every day.

7. Take good care of _____ typewriter.

   _____ typewriters are expensive.

8. Sandy likes to watch _____ television.

   _____ television at my house is broken.

9. Our friends live on _____ State Street.

   It's _____ street with the tall oak trees.

10. Where is _____ Amazon River?

    It's in _____ Brazil.

PUNCTUATION

Here are some basic rules for using commas:

1. Use commas to separate things in a series. The comma before the conjunction is optional.
   He likes cars, girls and rock music.
   She went home, took a shower, and changed her clothes.

2. Use a comma before a conjunction joining two independent clauses (compound sentences).
   He talked to Maria yesterday, and he told her everything.
   She listened to him, but she didn't believe him.

3. Use commas with dates and addresses.
   It happened on Saturday, July 9, 1975.   They live in Miami, Florida.

4. Use a comma after introductory words like *well, yes,* and *no.*
   No, I can't see you tonight.   Well, what do you think?

5. Use a comma before question tags.
   It's a beautiful day, isn't it?   You aren't leaving, are you?

i   *Punctuate the following sentences using commas, periods, and question marks.*

Example: Finally she sold her house and moved to Dallas Texas

Finally, she sold her house and moved to Dallas, Texas.

1. I bought some bread butter and eggs but I forgot the milk

   _____

2. Our neighbors are nice friendly people and they like children

   _____

3. They got married on June 20 1984

   _____

4. Well how do you like the apartment

   _____

5. We painted the kitchen repaired the roof and bought a new sofa

   _____

6. You're in a hurry aren't you

   _____

7. Oh all right you can take the car

   _____

CAPITALIZATION

Here are some basic rules for capital letters:

1. Use a capital letter to begin each sentence.
   She likes to study.

2. Use capitals for the names of specific persons, places, or things.
   Richard Nixon visited the Great Wall of China.

3. Capitalize the names of religions, nationalities, languages, and countries.
   In Brazil they speak Portuguese.   Most Brazilians are Catholics.

4. Capitalize the first and last words and all important words in titles.
   My favorite book is The Fall of the Roman Empire.

5. Capitalize the days of the week, the months of year, and the names of holidays.
   Do not capitalize the names of seasons.
   Monday, February 14th, is Valentine's Day.
   We usually have good weather in the spring.

j *Rewrite the following sentences. Put in the missing capital letters.*

Example: they're showing the adventures of tarzan at the rex theater.

They're showing the Adventures of Tarzan at the Rex Theater.

1. christopher colombus discovered america.

   _____

2. sunday, july 4th, is independence day.

   _____

3. last summer, the browns went to new york.

   _____

4. the song, twist and shout, was a big hit in england.

   _____

5. i really enjoyed the book, midnight in moscow.

   _____

6. maria miranda studied medicine at the university of paris.

   _____

7. her birthday is on wednesday, may 3rd.

   _____

k *The following sentences have mistakes in grammar or vocabulary. Find the mistakes and rewrite the sentences correctly.*

Examples: He ~~comes~~ (always) late to work. *He always comes late to work.*

She isn't doing ~~nothing~~. *She isn't doing anything.*

They didn't like the movie, ~~also~~. *They didn't like the movie, either.*

1. Me and Linda were at the party. _____

2. I don't like when they make noise. _____

3. He's not afraid of nobody. _____

4. She likes every week to play tennis. _____

5. Both of them didn't pass the test. _____

6. My brother has twenty years. _____

7. I'm going home after a few minutes. _____

8. Do you like to see my photographs? _____

9. She didn't call him and write to him. _____

10. We don't take breakfast every day. _____

l *Write original sentences using the following words.*

Example: until *The post office is open until five o'clock.*

1. only _____

2. weekend _____

3. something _____

4. borrow _____

5. without _____

6. much _____

7. terrible _____

8. both _____

9. invite _____

10. nobody _____

CHAPTER FIVE

Future with "will"   Would like a . . .
Shall (suggestions and offers) Would like to . . .

Future with WILL   Affirmative

He She I You We They	'll will	come tomorrow.

a   *Change the following sentences from the past to the future.*

Example: She went to the bank at two o'clock.

She'll go to the bank at two o'clock.

1.   He spent his vacation in Mexico.

_____

2.   He took his family with him.

_____

3.   They went to Acapulco.

_____

4.   They arrived on July tenth.

_____

5.   They stayed at the Plaza Hotel.

_____

6.   They were there for two weeks.

_____

7.   Everyone had a good time.

_____

8.   They returned to the United States on July twenty-fourth.

_____

9.   They remembered their Mexican holiday for a long time.

_____

b   Every day Mrs. Golo teaches at the Wickam Elementary School. This is the last day of school and Mrs. Golo is very happy. Next week she will be on vacation in Hawaii, and she won't do any of the things that she normally does. *Look at the pictures and write sentences about Mrs. Golo using **won't**.*

1. She gets up early every day.

But she won't get up early next week.

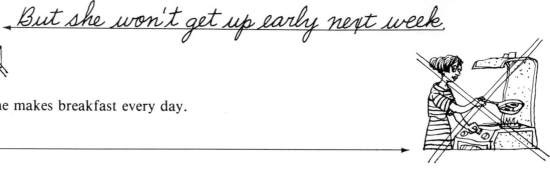

2. She makes breakfast every day.

_____

3. She reads the Wickam Daily News every day.

_____

4. She feeds the cat every day.

_____

5. She takes the bus every day.

_____

6. She goes to work every day.

_____

7. She teaches school every day.

_____

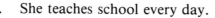

8. She talks to her students every day.

_____

WILL Negative

He She I You We They	won't (will not)	come today.

Interrogative

Will	he she I you we they	come tomorrow?

c   *Make questions as indicated.*

Example: She won't go to the market today.

Will she go to the market tomorrow?

1.   He won't go to work today.

_____

2.   They won't be here today.

_____

3.   We won't see them today.

_____

4.   He won't finish his homework today.

_____

5.   She won't clean the house today.

_____

6.   They won't wash the car today.

_____

7.   He won't help his sister today.

_____

8.   She won't make a cake today.

_____

9.   They won't paint the kitchen today.

_____

After class, Mrs. Golo will say goodbye to her students. . . .

d *Look at the pictures and write a short composition about Mrs. Golo, using the future tense with **will**. Use the words listed below.*

Mrs. Golo	say	put	goodbye	car	Hawaii
students	pick up	come	husband	neighbor	
Mr. Golo	feed	drive	cat	airport	
Mabel Brown	pack	take	suitcase	plane	
	leave				

Question with WOULD

| Would you like | a sandwich?
some tomato juice? |
| | to dance?
to play tennis? |

Short Answer

| Yes, I would. |

| No, I wouldn't. |

e *Make sentences using **would you like to**.*

Examples: My sister has some new records. (listen to)

Would you like to listen to them?

Peter is a good dancer. (dance)

Would you like to dance with him?

1. Those books are very interesting. (borrow)

_____

2. Maria is at home now. (call)

_____

3. There's a good movie at the Rex Cinema. (see)

_____

4. Dr. Pasto has a lot of interesting ideas. (talk to)

_____

5. There are some beautiful photographs on the desk. (look at)

_____

6. I like the large photograph of the dog. (have)

_____

7. Miss Jones can't carry all those boxes. (help)

_____

8. We got some letters from our friends. (read)

_____

9. My brother will be here this afternoon. (wait for)

_____

50

f *Write questions using would you like a/some.*

Examples: tea *Would you like some tea?*

banana *Would you like a banana?*

1. orange juice _____

2. bread _____

3. sandwich _____

4. dish of ice cream _____

5. cereal _____

6. glass of water _____

7. apple _____

8. cheese _____

9. bowl of soup _____

g *Rewrite the following sentences using contractions.*

Example: They would like to see a movie. *They'd like to see a movie.*

1. I would like to visit Australia. _____

2. She would like to learn Spanish. _____

3. He would like to study medicine. _____

4. They would like to have a car. _____

5. We would like to work at the museum. _____

6. You would like to find a good job. _____

7. She would like to buy a new dress. _____

8. I would like to read that book. _____

9. They would like to attend the meeting. _____

h *Write the past tense of the irregular verbs given below.*

Example: drive *drove*

1. leave _____
2. sit _____
3. come _____
4. do _____
5. take _____
6. have _____
7. buy _____
8. eat _____
9. see _____
10. drink _____
11. make _____
12. get _____
13. say _____
14. write _____
15. read _____
16. wear _____
17. think _____
18. stand _____

i *Complete the following sentences with suitable prepositions.*

Example: Barbara works *at* the bank *from* nine *to* five.

1. She gets up early _____ the morning and goes _____ work _____ bus.

2. Yesterday she talked _____ us _____ her job.

3. Peter danced _____ Maria _____ the party last night.

4. He's leaving _____ New York _____ seven o'clock _____ the morning.

5. There's a package here _____ you. It's _____ Mrs. Golo.

6. She went _____ Hawaii last week and left her cat _____ Mabel.

7. I stopped _____ Nancy's house on my way home _____ the office.

8. She lives _____ the corner _____ Maple Street and Third Avenue.

9. Nancy made a large pot _____ coffee _____ the two _____ us.

10. I took some cups _____ the shelf and put them _____ the table.

11. Nancy likes her coffee _____ cream and sugar. I never put anything _____ my coffee.

12. I stayed _____ Nancy's _____ a couple of hours. We had a nice time together.

52

j *Answer the following questions about yourself.*

1. How often do you go to the market?

_____

2. What kind of food do you buy?

_____

3. Do you prefer to eat at home or in a restaurant?

_____

4. How long does it take you to wash the dishes?

_____

5. What are you going to do this Saturday?

_____

6. What kind of weather do you like?

_____

7. What do you wear when you want to be comfortable?

_____

8. What are your neighbors like?

_____

9. Where did you live when you were a child?

_____

10. How did you have fun when you were a child?

_____

11. What do you like to do in your free time?

_____

12. How much time do you spend on the phone?

_____

13. What do you and your friends talk about?

_____

CHAPTER SIX

Object pronouns   **Too/enough**
Phrasal verbs

a *Look at the pictures and answer the questions using object pronouns.*

1. What's Tino buying <u>Barbara</u>?

   He's buying her some flowers.

2. What's Anne bringing <u>Mr. Bascomb</u>?

   She's bringing him some coffee.

3. What's Otis showing <u>the children</u>?

   ← _____

4. What's Albert taking <u>Linda</u>?

   _____ →

5. What's Mrs. Golo feeding <u>the cat</u>?

   ← _____

6. What's Mabel serving <u>her guests</u>?

   _____ →

7. What's Susie giving <u>the teacher</u>?

   ← _____

8. What's Johnnie selling <u>the old lady</u>?

   _____ →

Word Order with DIRECT and INDIRECT OBJECTS

Tom is	buying getting giving bringing	her him me you us them	the book.

He's	buying getting	it	for to	her. him. me. you. us. them.
	giving bringing			

b   *Rewrite the following sentences using object pronouns.*

Examples: I'm taking these letters to Barbara.

I'm taking them to her.

She's getting that tie for her boyfriend.

She's getting it for him.

1.   We're sending this package to the Browns.

_____

2.   I'm buying these magazines for Miss Jones.

_____

3.   She's saving those stamps for you and me.

_____

4.   We're giving this lamp to the neighbors.

_____

5.   They're selling the large painting to Mr. Bascomb.

_____

6.   He's repairing that clock for his wife.

_____

7.   She's getting the records for Nancy and me.

_____

8.   I'm giving these books to Sam.

_____

9.   He's taking the typewriter to Mr. and Mrs. Golo.

_____

c *Look at the pictures and answer the questions using phrasal verbs.*

1. What's Mr. Bascomb looking for?

    He's looking for his umbrella.

2. Who's Tino waiting for?

    He's waiting for Barbara.

3. What are the dogs running after?

    _____

4. What's Anne looking at?

    _____

5. What's Sam putting on?

    _____

6. What's Johnnie picking up?

    _____

7. What's Linda putting away?

    _____

8. What's Barbara trying on?

    _____

58

PHRASAL VERBS   Inseparable

| We're | looking <br> waiting | for | Maria.
 our friends. |

OBJECT PRONOUNS

| We're | looking <br> waiting | for | her.
 them. |

d   *Rewrite the following sentences using object pronouns:*

Example: We went over those reports. *We went over them.* _____

1.   She waited for Jimmy. _____

2.   He ran after his friends. _____

3.   They called on Mrs. Golo. _____

4.   She got over her illness. _____

5.   We looked at those magazines. _____

6.   I ran into Miss Jones. _____

7.   She stood up for her little brother. _____

8.   He got through his homework. _____

PHRASAL VERBS   Separable

| He's | picking up <br> putting away | the newspaper.
 the magazines. |

OBJECT PRONOUNS

| He's | picking it up.
 putting them away. |

e   *Rewrite the following sentences using object pronouns.*

Examples: He called up Maria. *He called her up.* _____

She tried on the yellow dress. *She tried it on.* _____

1.   He fixed up his apartment. _____

2.   She took off her shoes. _____

3.   They put away the dishes. _____

4.   I paid back my father. _____

5.   He put off the meeting. _____

6.   We looked up Miss Sherman. _____

7.   She called up her boyfriend. _____

8.   He took back the books. _____

f *Look at the pictures and answer the questions using **too** or **enough**.*

1. Why can't Albert be on the track team?

   He's too slow. (He isn't fast enough.)

2. Why can't Tino wear that shirt?

   It's too dirty. (It isn't clean enough.)

3. Why can't Linda finish her homework?

   _____

4. Why can't Marty pick the oranges?

   _____

5. Why doesn't Mrs. Golo like her dinner?

   _____

6. Why can't Johnnie lift the chair?

   _____

7. Why can't Peter's car hold four people?

   _____

8. Why can't Fred hear Barney?

   _____

60

ENOUGH

Mrs. Golo doesn't have enough	time to go to the library. energy to clean the house. strength to lift that table.

TOO

She's too	busy (to go to the library). tired (to clean the house). weak (to lift that table).

g *Write sentences with too.*

Examples: My little brother isn't big enough to play football.

<u>*He's too small to play football.*</u>

That dog isn't smart enough to learn anything.

<u>*It's too dumb to learn anything.*</u>

1. Marty isn't tall enough to pick those oranges.

_____

2. The oranges aren't ripe enough to eat.

_____

3. Your sister isn't pretty enough to be an actress.

_____

4. That car isn't big enough to hold five people.

_____

5. Albert isn't fast enough to be a good tennis player.

_____

6. Some men aren't smart enough to save their money.

_____

7. That jacket isn't clean enough to wear to the party.

_____

8. Jimmy isn't old enough to drive a car.

_____

9. You aren't strong enough to lift those boxes.

_____

h *What do you think is going to happen? Make sentences using **going to**.*

Example: Jimmy is going to the post office. *He's going to mail a letter.*

OR *He's going to buy some stamps.*

1. Linda is going to the library. _____

2. Albert is opening the refrigerator door. _____

3. Barbara is looking for the shampoo. _____

4. Tino is walking to the flower shop. _____

5. Anne is putting some paper in the typewriter. _____

6. Jack is opening a can of dog food. _____

7. Barney is going to the bank. _____

8. The girls are looking at the cinema guide. _____

9. Peter is picking up the phone. _____

10. Maria is running the bath water. _____

11. Sam is going to the drugstore. _____

12. Mabel is putting some plates on the table. _____

i *Write original sentences using the adverbs given below.*

Examples: hard *I work hard.* _____

slowly *My mother drives slowly.* _____

1. well _____

2. badly _____

3. fast _____

4. slowly _____

5. carefully _____

6. hard _____

7. loudly _____

8. quickly _____

9. beautifully _____

j *Complete the following sentences with the words indicated, with or without **the**.*

Example: girls

(a) Jimmy likes _*girls*_ .

(b) _*The girls*_ at Jimmy's school think he's cute.

1. bread

(a) _____ in France is very good.

(b) What kind of _____ do you like?

2. bananas

(a) _____ are usually cheap.

(b) _____ in that market are expensive.

3. furniture

(a) I like _____ in your apartment.

(b) Where is a good place to buy _____ ?

4. water

(a) Plants need _____ to grow.

(b) Is it safe to drink _____ in Cuba?

5. tomatoes

(a) Do you like _____ ?

(b) _____ in my garden are very large.

6. apples

(a) Where did you put _____ ?

(b) _____ are good for you.

7. food

(a) I don't like _____ at Joe's Cafe.

(b) Do you spend much money on _____ ?

8. history

(a) My favorite subject is _____ .

(b) I want to study _____ of Mexico.

9. cigarettes

(a) Did you take _____ that were on the table?

(b) _____ are bad for you.

CHAPTER SEVEN

Ago/how long ago?   **Past continuous**
Must (obligation)

a   *It's ten o'clock in the morning. Look at the pictures and answer the questions using* **ago.**

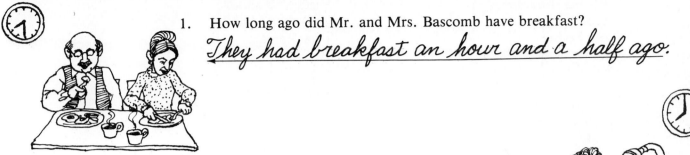

1. How long ago did Mr. and Mrs. Bascomb have breakfast?

They had breakfast an hour and a half ago.

2. How long ago did Anne take a shower?

_____

3. How long ago did Albert call Linda?

4. How long ago did Jimmy and Linda wash the dishes?

_____

5. How long ago did Barbara take the bus?

6. How long ago did she get to work?

_____

7. How long ago did Sam leave the house?

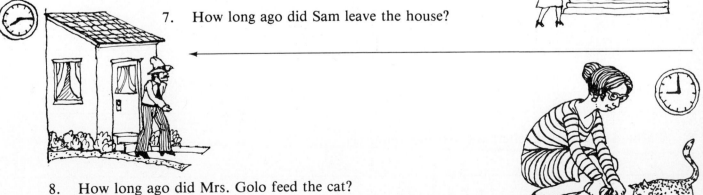

8. How long ago did Mrs. Golo feed the cat?

_____

HOW LONG AGO?

Mr. Brown	left his shop. took the bus. got home. had dinner.

How long ago did he	leave his shop? take the bus? get home? have dinner?

b   *Make questions with **how long ago**.*

Examples: Mabel went to the market.

How long ago did she go to the market?

She made dinner.

How long ago did she make dinner?

1.   Mrs. Golo called the theater.

_____

2.   Her husband took a shower.

_____

3.   They went to the movies.

_____

4.   Jimmy finished his homework.

_____

5.   Linda received the package.

_____

6.   They spoke to Mrs. Golo.

_____

7.   Dr. Pasto visited Colombia.

_____

8.   He met the president.

_____

9.   Barbara typed those letters for Mr. Bascomb.

_____

c *Write dialogues about the pictures, as indicated.*

1. A: *I saw Ula Hackey at the Rex Theater yesterday.*
   B: *What was she doing?*
   A: *She was signing autographs.*

Ula Hackey

2. A: *I saw Otis and Gloria at the park yesterday.*
   B: *What were they doing?*
   A: *They were riding their bicycles.*

Otis and Gloria

3. A: _____
   _____
   B: _____
   A: _____

Albert

4. A: _____
   _____
   B: _____
   A: _____

Barbara and Tino

5. A: _____

    _____

  B: _____

  A: _____

6. A: _____

    _____

  B: _____

  A: _____

7. A: _____

    _____

  B: _____

  A: _____

8. A: _____

    _____

  B: _____

  A: _____

PAST CONTINUOUS   Affirmative

He She I	was	sleeping working	when the telephone rang.
You We They	were	reading studying	while it was raining.

d   *Write sentences using the past continuous with **while**.*

Examples: Jimmy / swimming—Albert / lying on the beach

Jimmy was swimming while Albert was lying on the beach.

We / washing the dishes—you / cleaning the windows

We were washing the dishes while you were cleaning the windows

1. Mr. and Mrs. Bascomb / dancing—Dr. Pasto / playing the piano

   _____

2. I / writing some letters—my sister / preparing dinner

   _____

3. Mrs. Golo / visiting her brother—we / attending the lecture

   _____

4. Jimmy / helping his father—Linda / resting in the back yard

   _____

5. They / doing their homework—it / raining outside

   _____

6. Mabel / eating breakfast—Sam / reading the newspaper

   _____

7. We / listening to the radio—he / repairing his car

   _____

8. Albert / taking a shower—his friends / waiting in the living room

   _____

9. They / playing chess—you / sleeping on the couch

   _____

e *Complete the following sentences using the past continuous and the past simple:*

Examples:

Barbara (sit) *was sitting* in a restaurant when she (meet) *met* Tino.

We (watch) *were watching* television when our friends (arrive) *arrived*.

1. Otis (dance) _____ with Gloria when the music (stop) _____.

2. I (play) _____ cards when they (walk) _____ into the room.

3. Nancy (wait for) _____ the bus when Barney (pull up) _____ in his taxi.

4. We (think) _____ of you when we (get) _____ your letter.

5. Mr. Bascomb (leave) _____ the office when his wife (call) _____.

6. They (walk) _____ in the park when they (run) _____ into an old friend.

7. Jack (read) _____ a book when an old lady (come) _____ and (sit) _____ next to him.

8. The Golos (eat) _____ dinner when the phone (ring) _____.

f *Make questions with **who**, **what**, or **where**.*

Examples: Otis and Gloria were at Joe's Cafe. *Where were they?*

They were listening to Barney. *Who were they listening to?*

He was talking about football. *What was he talking about?*

1. Jack was at the garage. _____

2. He was repairing his car. _____

3. He was getting help from Nick. _____

4. The children were standing by the door. _____

5. They were waiting for Mr. Poole. _____

6. He was reading a letter. _____

7. Albert was at the park. _____

8. He was taking pictures of Jimmy and Linda. _____

9. They were wearing cowboy hats. _____

g   *Write a short composition about this picture using the past continuous.*

boy	wait	sell	ledge	book
girl	stand	play	snack bar	newspaper
young man	sit	eat	bench	sandwich
young woman	clean	smoke	bus stop	pipe
old man	read	talk	window	dog
old ladies	buy			
workmen				

72

h *Complete the following sentences using the most appropriate phrasal verb from the list below. Each verb may be used only once.*

try on	be back	pay back	fix up
look over	pick up	take up	turn off
call on	take off	get off	come in

Examples: Jimmy is going to *pick up* _____ a package at the post office.

He'll *get off* _____ the bus at the next stop.

1. Barney wants to _____ his car. He's having trouble with the engine.

2. Mabel went to the market. She'll _____ in an hour.

3. Is it O.K. if I _____ these reports?

4. Please _____ the lights when you leave the room.

5. When are you going to _____ Mr. Bascomb? He wants his money.

6. I'm going to _____ him this afternoon. He's expecting me.

7. Linda wants to _____ the dress before she buys it.

8. Open the door. Somebody wants to _____.

9. _____ that hat! It looks terrible on you.

10. You need some exercise. Are you going to _____ a sport this summer?

i *Complete the following sentences using **very** or **too**.*

Examples: The table is *very* _____ expensive, but I'm going to buy it.

The desk is *too* _____ expensive for me. I can't buy it.

1. Dr. Pasto is a _____ intelligent man.

2. Barbara is _____ tired to play tennis today.

3. That car is _____ old, but it runs well.

4. I don't think this book is _____ difficult for you.

5. This coffee is _____ hot to drink.

6. Tino is _____ strong, but he can't lift that table.

7. Maria bought the dress on sale. It was _____ cheap.

8. Johnnie can't wear that coat. It's _____ small for him.

CHAPTER EIGHT

Review

a *Yesterday some strange things were happening at the Cafe of the Absurd. Look at the picture and complete the sentences using the past continuous.*

Examples: A duck *was reading* a newspaper.

Two women *were armwrestling* .

1. The chef _____ for the customers.

2. A policeman _____ the violin.

3. Two cats _____ to the music.

4. The waitress _____ a unicycle.

5. A cowboy and an Indian _____ cards.

6. A dog _____ beer.

7. Two bums _____ hot dogs.

8. A woman _____ her teeth.

9. A monkey _____ a picture of the cafe.

76

b *Write sentences using* **enough.**

Examples: Tino is very strong. He can lift almost anything.

He's strong enough to lift almost anything.

Albert is twenty years old. He can vote.

He's old enough to vote.

1. Albert is very hungry. He's going to eat four hamburgers.

_____

2. He's thirsty, too. He's going to drink five glasses of milk.

_____

3. Jimmy is smart. He plans to go to the University.

_____

4. Mabel is very energetic. She likes to work in the garden every day.

_____

5. Linda is nineteen years old. She can drive a car.

_____

6. Mr. Bascomb is rich. He can buy almost anything.

_____

7. Barbara is very lucky. She can have everything she wants.

_____

8. Maria is very nice. She tries to help everyone.

_____

9. Mr. Bascomb's car is big. It can hold six people.

_____

10. Your sister is strong. She can carry her own suitcase.

_____

c *Complete the following sentences using* **can, can't, will, won't, shall, would,** *and* **must.**

Example: Nobody ___*can*___ tell him anything. He ___*won't*___ listen.

1. My brother is coming for dinner. He _____ be here at six o'clock.

2. Fred never works. He _____ be lazy.

3. It's a beautiful day. _____ we go to the park?

4. You look hungry. _____ you like something to eat?

5. Susie _____ go to the movies because she has to do her homework.

6. Unfortunately, she _____ have time to see her friends today.

7. It's hot in here. _____ I open the window?

8. Our neighbors are always on the phone. They _____ like to talk.

9. Dr. Pasto is very intelligent. He _____ discuss anything.

10. Do you think it _____ rain tomorrow?

11. I _____ like to visit Japan someday.

12. Barbara is a good tennis player. She _____ practice a lot.

13. I have a guitar but I _____ play it very well.

14. There isn't any food in the refrigerator. _____ we go to the market?

15. Hurry up. I'm afraid we _____ be late for the meeting.

16. My sister _____ talk to that boy because she doesn't like him.

17. Albert has a big appetite. He _____ eat four hamburgers.

18. _____ you like to see a movie tonight?

d *Write the past tense of the irregular verbs given below.*

1. tell *told*
2. meet _____
3. speak _____
4. win _____
5. forget _____
6. bring _____

7. lose _____
8. find _____
9. swim _____
10. ride _____
11. give _____
12. fly _____

13. sell _____
14. teach _____
15. hear _____
16. sleep _____
17. feel _____
18. run _____

78

e *Complete the following sentences with suitable verbs in the past continuous.*

Examples: We *were leaving the office* _____ when she called.

He *was driving to work* _____ when he had an accident.

1. She _____ when he came into the room.

2. I _____ when I heard a loud noise.

3. He _____ when the telephone rang.

4. They _____ when the package arrived.

5. We _____ when it started to rain.

6. He _____ when he lost his keys.

7. She _____ when she saw the bandits.

8. I _____ when they left.

f *Complete the following sentences using **and, or, but, because, so, although,** and **besides.***

Examples: Sam doesn't make much money *although* _____ he works very hard.

Barbara doesn't have a car, ___*so*___ she takes the bus to work.

1. Linda can't go out today _____ she has to do her homework.

2. Jack knows a lot about sports _____ politics.

3. Sam is too tired to work in the garden. _____, he wants to watch the football game on TV.

4. I'd like to paint the living room, _____ I don't have enough time.

5. Mrs. Hamby is trying to lose weight, _____ she eats very little.

6. Johnnie doesn't like football _____ basketball.

7. Nancy seldom has visitors _____ she's very sociable.

8. Mr. Bascomb didn't go to work yesterday _____ he was sick.

9. You can come to the party, _____ don't bring your sister.

10. I don't want to see her _____ talk to her.

11. Otis is a vegetarian, _____ he doesn't eat meat.

12. Apples are delicious _____ they're good for you.

© 1988 Harcourt Brace Jovanovich, Inc. All rights reserved.

INDEFINITE ARTICLES VS. DEFINITE ARTICLE

The difference between **a/an** and **the**:

a/an means ''one of a class''   **the** means ''the one you and I know about''

Compare: **A** singer must have a good voice. (any singer, anyone of that profession)
The singer we heard last night was excellent. (you know which one: the singer we
heard last night)

Observe: He works in **a** small office on **the** sixth floor of **an** old building near **the** center of town.

a small office: there are several small offices—we don't know which one
an old building: there are a lot of old buildings—we don't know which one
the sixth floor: we know which floor—the sixth floor
the center of town: the town has only one center

Do not use **a/an** or **the** with these expressions:

to/at/from work	to/at/from school/college	to/at/from church	at home	at night
to/in/out of bed	for/at breakfast/lunch/dinner		by car/bus/bicycle/plane/train/boat

g   *Insert a, an, or the if necessary.*

Examples: She ordered __*a*__ hamburger and _____ French fries. *The* hamburger cost two

dollars, and *the* French fries were seventy-five cents.

1. _____ food at Mom's Cafe is terrific. I'm taking _____ friend to Mom's for _____ lunch.

2. "Do you know _____ good place to get _____ haircut?"

"_____ best place is Stanley's Barber Shop on _____ Main Street."

3. I saw _____ attractive woman standing at _____ bus stop in front of _____ Grand Hotel. She

was wearing _____ gray hat and _____ black shoes.

4. _____ man next door likes to write about _____ animals. Last week he wrote _____ short story

about _____ day in _____ life of _____ cat.

5. Sam bought _____ shirt and _____ tie. _____ shirt was cheap, but _____ tie was expensive.

6. "When was _____ last time you went to _____ beach?"

"_____ month ago. I went with my sister and we had _____ wonderful time."

7. We saw _____ old movie at _____ Rex Theater. It was about _____ love and _____ money.

8. _____ house at _____ end of _____ street belongs to Mr. Cooper. It's _____ beautiful house,

with _____ large windows and _____ red roof.

9. Mr. Cooper is _____ family man. He has _____ wife and three children. He's at _____ home

now, working in _____ garden. He's planting _____ vegetables.

h *Rewrite the following sentences. Put in the missing punctuation and capital letters.*

Example: ed's dog brutus is very mean and everyone's afraid of him

Ed's dog, Brutus, is very mean, and everyone's afraid of him.

1. there are many races nationalities and religions in the united states

_____

2. do most americans go to church on sunday

_____

3. last spring we went to yellowstone national park and it was wonderful

_____

4. the museum of natural history is next to the post office isn't it

_____

5. no it's across the street from the palace hotel

_____

6. unfortunately you can't visit the museum because it's closed today

_____

7. mabel went to al's market to buy some flour sugar eggs and chocolate

_____

8. she's going to make a chocolate cake for sam's birthday tomorrow

_____

9. we're going to have a party at the disco club on saturday august 20

_____

10. jane mary and alice are coming to the party with their boyfriends

_____

11. mary's boyfriend tom is from alabama

_____

12. he can sing and play the guitar but he can't dance

_____

i   *Complete the following sentences.*

Example: I think *the dog needs a bath.*

1. Would you like to _____

2. Is it true that _____

3. I was surprised when _____

4. He doesn't plan to _____

5. Why didn't you _____

6. She can't go out because _____

7. It's not my fault that _____

8. When was the last time _____

9. From now on, _____

10. I'm glad _____

11. Can they afford _____

12. You're lucky _____

j   *Write sentences about yourself using adverbs of frequency.*

Examples: sometimes *I sometimes drink coffee in the morning.*

hardly ever *I hardly ever watch television.*

1. often _____

2. never _____

3. usually _____

4. sometimes _____

5. always _____

6. seldom _____

7. normally _____

8. hardly ever _____

82

TAG QUESTIONS

It's a beautiful day,	isn't it?
They're going to the beach,	aren't they?
You have an umbrella,	don't you?
She was at the movies,	wasn't she?
He can play the piano,	can't he?

There aren't any matches,	are there?
He isn't working today,	is he?
They don't like football,	do they?
You weren't at the party,	were you?
She can't drive a truck,	can she?

k *Add question tags to the following sentences.*

Examples: Gloria is leaving the office at five o'clock.

Gloria is leaving the office at five o'clock, isn't she?

She doesn't want to walk home.

She doesn't want to walk home, does she?

1. Tino stopped at the garage last night.

   _____

2. Nick and Barney were there.

   _____

3. Barney was listening to the football game.

   _____

4. It wasn't a very interesting game.

   _____

5. They're going to the beach this weekend.

   _____

6. You don't think it will rain.

   _____

7. Barbara can't go to the beach.

   _____

8. She has to do some work this weekend.

   _____

9. It's a shame.

   _____

l *Complete the following sentences using* **some, any, one,** *and* **it.**

Examples: I need a dictionary. I'm going to buy __*one*__ tomorrow.

How much did you pay for your watch? Was __*it*__ very expensive?

Don't eat all the ice cream! Leave __*some*__ for me.

1. Ed needs some money. He doesn't have _____ .

2. Our neighbors aren't going to buy a television. They don't want _____ .

3. I saw a lot of movies last year. _____ were good and _____ were terrible.

4. Where's the radio? Is _____ in the car?

5. Linda used all the shampoo. She didn't leave _____ for Jimmy.

6. If there's no milk on the table, you can find _____ in the refrigerator.

7. Give me the newspaper. I want to read _____ .

8. There are two lamps. _____ is yellow and the other is green.

9. That soup looks good, but I don't want _____ .

10. Susie loves chocolate candy. She's going to buy _____ at the market.

m *Write original sentences using the following words.*

Example: downtown *I like to go shopping downtown.* _____

1. follow _____

2. plenty _____

3. anything _____

4. belong _____

5. enough _____

6. probably _____

7. about _____

8. none _____

9. refuse _____

10. everyone _____

84

n *Change the story about the party to the past tense.*

It's Saturday night and there's a big party at the Disco Club. Everyone is having a good time. The band is playing an old hit called *Twist and Shout*. Otis and Gloria are dancing to the music, and Johnnie is watching them. Peter and Maria are at the edge of the dance floor. They're holding hands and talking about their favorite songs. Barney is standing next to a table with a lot of food on it. He's eating potato chips and drinking lemonade. Barbara and Tino are sitting at a table in the corner. Barbara is wearing a beautiful dress. She's smiling at Tino, and he's laughing about something. Everyone is happy. It's a great party.

Last Saturday night there was a big party at the Disco Club. When we got there, everyone

was having a good time.

_____

_____

_____

_____

_____

_____

_____

_____

o *Complete the following sentences using these words:* **on, out, off, back, up.**

Example: Can you turn the radio *up* ? I can't hear it.

1. I don't like these magazines. I'm going to throw them _____ .

2. If you're so hot, why don't you take your coat _____ ?

3. Would you please put _____ your cigarette? The smoke is bothering me.

4. I like that hat. I want to try it _____ .

5. Can you loan me ten dollars? I'll pay you _____ tomorrow.

6. It's a little dark in here. Would you turn the light _____ , please?

7. We have to fix _____ our apartment. It's in bad condition.

8. Let's do it now and not put it _____ .

9. I'm going to take this defective lamp _____ to the store where I bought it.

10. When they sell you something that's no good, they have to give you your money _____ .

CHAPTER NINE

Comparative

a *Look at the pictures and write a sentence for each one using the comparative form.*

1. strong   *Tino is stronger than Johnnie.*

Tino   Johnnie

2. expensive   *A motorcycle is more expensive than a bicycle.*

$950 $75

a motorcycle   a bicycle

3. fashionable _____

Jane   Nancy

4. tall _____

Dr. Pasto   Mr. Bascomb

5. energetic _____

Jack

Sam

6. big _____

a Cadillac   a Volkswagen

7. heavy _____

8. comfortable _____

Albert   Jimmy

Mabel

Mrs. Golo

88

SHORT-WORD COMPARATIVE

He's	older stronger	than his friend.

He's	bigger fatter	than his friend.

She's	prettier friendlier	than her sister.

Irregular

Your	typewriter dictionary	is	better worse	than mine.

LONG-WORD COMPARATIVE

Their car is	more	expensive powerful	than ours.
	less	economical practical	

b   *Make questions as indicated.*

Examples: The Volkswagen and the Fiat are both good cars.

Which one is better?

Mr. Bascomb and Mrs. Smith are both ambitious.

Which one is more ambitious?

1.   Nick and Tino are both strong.

_____

2.   Nancy and Maria are both intelligent.

_____

3.   Mr. and Mrs. Golo are both careful drivers.

_____

4.   New York and Tokyo are both big cities.

_____

5.   Basketball and football are both popular sports.

_____

6.   Barbara and Tino are both athletic.

_____

7.   Albert and his father are both short.

_____

8.   Mrs. Brown and Mrs. Hamby are both fat.

_____

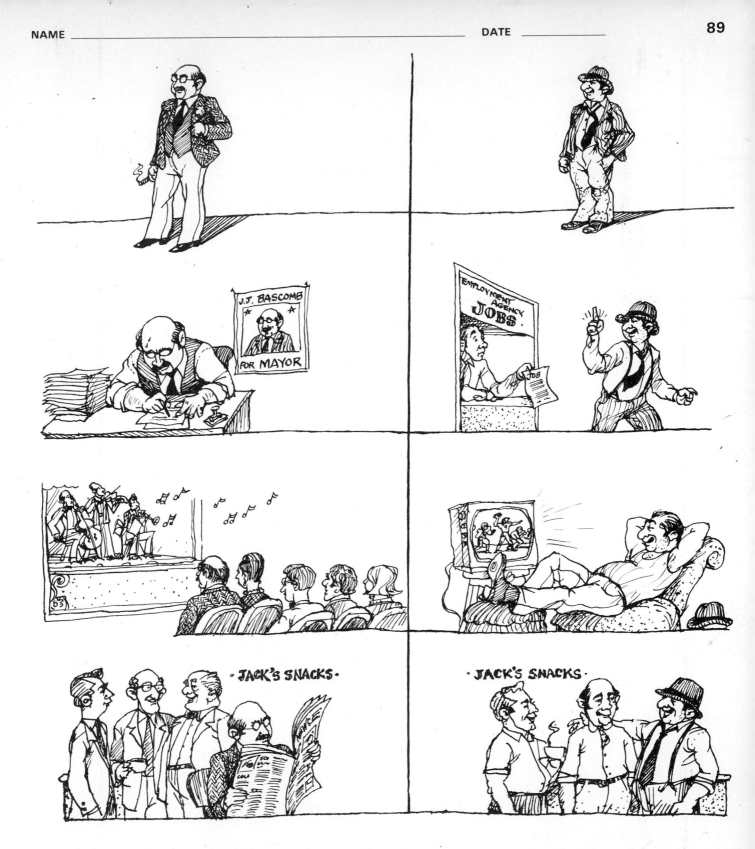

c *Look at the pictures on this page and write a short composition comparing Mr. Bascomb with Fred.*

busy	lazy	serious	fashionable
happy	friendly	intelligent	sophisticated
nice	popular	industrious	interesting

90

d   *Make comparisons using the adjectives listed below.*

Examples: tall   *My brother is taller than I am.*

expensive   *A car is more expensive than a bicycle.*

1. good _____

2. young _____

3. interesting _____

4. busy _____

5. athletic _____

6. fast _____

7. bad _____

8. difficult _____

9. cheap _____

e   *Complete the following sentences using these words:* **age, height, weight, size, price, color, speed, strength, population,** *and* **mileage.**

Example: Brazil is about the same *size* as the United States.

1. I bought a yellow lamp. Yellow is my favorite _____.

2. I paid five dollars for it. That's a good _____.

3. Mrs. Hamby eats very little. She's watching her _____.

4. How old is she? Do you know her _____?

5. Nick and Tino are both six feet tall. They're the same _____.

6. Tino can lift anything. His _____ is incredible.

7. His car can travel thirty miles on a gallon of gas. That's good _____.

8. It can go 120 miles an hour. That's the maximum _____.

9. Sao Paulo has more than twelve million people and the _____ is growing.

f   *Complete the following sentences using suitable prepositions.*

Example: I like to watch TV _*until*_ late _*at*_ night.

1.   Linda lives _____ her family _____ a small house _____ State Street.

2.   She came _____ the living room and put some flowers _____ the table.

3.   She moved the bookcase _____ the bedroom _____ the living room.

4.   The dictionary is _____ the top shelf _____ the bookcase.

5.   Peter is talking _____ his girlfriend _____ the phone.

6.   He's taking her _____ a party _____ the Plaza Hotel.

7.   Wait for me _____ the corner _____ Lime Street and Third Avenue.

8.   Don't worry _____ your friends, we'll see them later.

9.   We'll stay _____ the hotel _____ the end _____ the party.

g   *Make original sentences using the following verbs + infinitive.*

Examples: like _*I like to read.*_

refuse _*She refused to eat her dinner.*_

1.   learn _____

2.   forget _____

3.   try _____

4.   hope _____

5.   decide _____

6.   want _____

7.   expect _____

8.   love _____

9.   hate _____

92

h *Rewrite the following sentences using the adverbs indicated.*

Examples: (perhaps) She's at the library. *Perhaps she's at the library.*

(there) She works in the morning. *She works there in the morning.*

(quickly) She can type. *She can type quickly.*

1. (often) He walked by my house. _____

2. (here) He came last week. _____

3. (closely) We watched him. _____

4. (quickly) He ran down the street. _____

5. (anywhere) I can't find my money. _____

6. (perhaps) He took the money. _____

7. (soon) I hope the police will come. _____

8. (hard) I worked for that money. _____

9. (again) I saw him last Sunday. _____

10. (unfortunately) I don't remember his name. _____

11. (always) He wears a black hat. _____

12. (then) I had his address and I lost it. _____

13. (probably) He's in Mexico now. _____

14. (well) He speaks Spanish. _____

15. (maybe) He learned it in school. _____

i *Write original sentences using the adverbs given below.*

Example: usually *I usually take the bus to work.*

1. perhaps _____

2. carefully _____

3. soon _____

4. somewhere _____

5. never _____

j *Complete the following dialogue with the missing verb forms.*

GLORIA: How ___*are*___ you ___*going*___ home today, Sandy?
(go)

SANDY: I _____ home.
(walk)

GLORIA: You normally _____ the bus, don't you?
(take)

SANDY: Yes, but today I have to _____ at the market and _____ some food
(stop)   (get)

for dinner.

GLORIA: Which market _____ you _____ to?
(go)

SANDY: The one on State Street. They _____ a sale this week.
(have)

GLORIA: I know. I _____ there last night and _____ some hot dogs. I also
(go)   (buy)

_____ some paper plates and cups.
(get)

SANDY: _____ you _____ a picnic?
(have)

GLORIA: Yes, tomorrow at City Park. Would you like _____ ?
(come)

SANDY: Sure. That _____ fun. Who else _____ ?
(be)   (come)

GLORIA: Everyone. Even Peter _____ there.
(be)

SANDY: Oh, Gloria. That's wonderful. When did you _____ Peter?
(invite)

GLORIA: Last night. I _____ him as I _____ the market. He _____
(see)   (leave)   (walk)

down the street with Maria.

SANDY: With Maria? _____ she _____ to the picnic, too?
(go)

GLORIA: I _____ so. She and Peter _____ about it when I _____
(think)   (talk)   (leave)

them.

SANDY: Gloria, on second thought, I don't think I _____ to the picnic tomorrow.
(go)

I have to _____ some work around the house and besides, I think it
(do)

_____ tomorrow.
(rain)

k *Make questions with **who**, **what**, or **where**.*

Examples: Sam wants to live on a farm. *Where does he want to live ?*

He was talking to his real estate agent. *Who was he talking to ?*

They were looking at some photographs. *What were they looking at?*

1. Gloria is talking to Sandy. _____

2. She has to go to the market. _____

3. She has to buy some food. _____

4. The market is on State Street. _____

5. Gloria bought some hot dogs. _____

6. She saw Peter in front of the market. _____

7. He was walking with Maria. _____

8. They were talking about the picnic. _____

9. The picnic will be at City Park. _____

l *Choose an adverb of frequency and write a true sentence about yourself.*

Example: busy on the weekend *I'm usually busy on the weekend.*

OR *I'm never busy on the weekend.*

1. tired in the morning _____

2. in a hurry _____

3. late to class _____

4. free in the afternoon _____

5. at home in the evening _____

6. in bed by midnight _____

CHAPTER TEN

Present perfect: regular and irregular verbs

Present perfect/ past simple contrast

Present perfect with ''for'' and ''since''

PRESENT PERFECT Affirmative

He She	's (has)	taken a shower. had breakfast.
I You We They	've (have)	washed the dishes. cleaned the kitchen.

a *Complete the following sentences using the present perfect (regular verbs).*

Examples: We '*ve planted* some tomatoes in the garden. (plant)

He '*s looked at* all the magazines on the desk. (look at)

1. She _____ in France and England. (live)

2. He _____ to some famous people. (talk)

3. They _____ many interesting places. (visit)

4. We _____ to visit Mexico for a long time. (want)

5. She _____ in several movies. (appear)

6. They _____ five letters this week. (receive)

7. I _____ to look for a job. (decide)

8. You _____ me a lot recently. (help)

b *Complete the following sentences using the present perfect (irregular verbs).*

Examples: I '*ve been* to his apartment twice this week. (be)

He '*s shown* me most of his paintings. (show)

1. She _____ the office. (leave)

2. She _____ her keys. (forget)

3. I _____ some good books this month. (read)

4. We _____ a lot about the future. (think)

5. He _____ his stamp collection. (sell)

6. She _____ the same dress three times this week. (wear)

7. I _____ her for a long time. (know)

8. She _____ a lot of interesting things in her life. (do)

PRESENT PERFECT   Negative

He She	hasn't (has not)	taken a shower. had breakfast.
I You We They	haven't (have not)	washed the dishes. cleaned the kitchen.

Interrogative

Has	he she	taken a shower? had breakfast?
Have	I you we they	washed the dishes? cleaned the kitchen?

c   *Make negative sentences using the present perfect.*

Examples: We've cleaned the kitchen. (the living room)

But we haven't cleaned the living room.

She's found her handbag. (her keys)

But she hasn't found her keys.

1.   He's visited Japan. (Australia)

_____

2.   They've spoken to Peter. (Maria)

_____

3.   I've written to my brother. (my sister)

_____

4.   She's learned to play volleyball. (tennis)

_____

5.   He's worked at the post office. (the bank)

_____

6.   You've shown me your record player. (your new camera)

_____

7.   We've talked about football. (basketball)

_____

8.   I've fed the dog. (the cat)

_____

9.   Linda's tried on the yellow hat. (the green hat)

_____

d   *Make questions using the present perfect.*

Examples: you/see/that movie   *Have you seen that movie?*

he/arrive/the hotel   *Has he arrived at the hotel?*

1.   she/go/the market _____

2.   you / eat / Joe's Cafe _____

3.   he/fix up/his apartment _____

4.   she/clean/the kitchen _____

5.   they/save/their money _____

6.   you/call/the office _____

7.   he/sell/his watch _____

8.   she/write/her father _____

9.   they/leave/the hotel _____

e   *Make questions with **who, what,** and **where**.*

Examples: He's spoken to Linda.   *Who has he spoken to?*

She's done her homework.   *What has she done?*

They've gone to the movies.   *Where have they gone?*

1.   She's met Dr. Pasto. _____

2.   She's been to his house. _____

3.   She's read his books. _____

4.   He's lived in Egypt and India. _____

5.   He's studied several languages. _____

6.   He's worked with Sy Polanski. _____

7.   Our friends have sold their house. _____

8.   They've gone to Chicago. _____

9.   They've written to my sister. _____

PRESENT PERFECT with FOR and SINCE

They've (They have)	worked lived	in Wickam City	for	several weeks. a few months. a long time.
			since	January. last year. 1985.

f   *Answer the following questions using the present perfect with **for** or **since**.*

Examples: How long have they worked in the movies? (several years)

They've worked in the movies for several years.

How long has she played tennis? (last year)

She's played tennis since last year.

1.   How long has he had a motorcycle? (last winter)

_____

2.   How long has she been a secretary? (a couple of years)

_____

3.   How long have they lived at the same address? (1965)

_____

4.   How long have they known Mr. Bascomb? (six months)

_____

5.   How long has the bank been open today? (half an hour)

_____

6.   How long has she worked at the market? (last summer)

_____

7.   How long has he driven a taxi? (a long time)

_____

8.   How long have they listened to jazz? (many years)

_____

9.   How long has she studied music? (high school)

_____

g *Complete the following sentences using the past simple or the present perfect.*

Examples:

Mr. and Mrs. Golo (move) *moved* into their new apartment last summer.

Since then they (meet) *have met* most of the people in their building.

1. Barney (be) _____ a taxi driver for several years.

2. He (fix up) _____ his taxi a few weeks ago.

3. Maria (receive) _____ three letters last week.

4. She (receive) _____ only one letter this week.

5. Peter (meet) _____ some old friends at the airport this morning.

6. He (be) _____ with them since nine o'clock.

7. They (have) _____ breakfast a little while ago.

8. I (see) _____ that movie three times.

9. I (see) _____ it the first time when I (be) _____ in high school.

h *Make negative questions as indicated.*

Examples: Have you eaten dinner? *Haven't you eaten dinner?*

Are you hungry? *Aren't you hungry?*

1. Did you see Nick yesterday? _____

2. Was he at the garage? _____

3. Are your friends having a picnic? _____

4. Will Linda be there? _____

5. Did you tell her about the picnic? _____

6. Do you have her telephone number? _____

7. Can you get it for me? _____

8. Has anyone seen my hat? _____

9. Is it in the living room? _____

102

i   *Complete the following sentences.*

Examples: He doesn't have a car, but she _*does*_.

We've visited the museum, but they _*haven't*_.

I'm busy right now, but you _*aren't*_.

1.   She can swim, but he _____.

2.   He isn't very athletic, but she _____.

3.   They didn't enjoy the party, but we _____.

4.   I'm not a very good dancer, but I think you _____.

5.   He likes to go out, but she _____.

6.   He's seen that movie, but she _____.

7.   You haven't eaten at Joe's Cafe, but I _____.

8.   We were having a good time last night, but they _____.

9.   They don't like loud music and hot food, but we _____.

10.   She wasn't in a very good mood, but I _____.

11.   He'll listen to me, but she _____.

12.   He's my friend, but she _____.

j   *Find the words that have similar meanings and fill in the blanks below.*

sociable	difficult	stupid	modern
amusing	quick	ordinary	different
large	begin	terrible	intelligent

1.   fast _*quick*_

2.   smart _____

3.   funny _____

4.   dumb _____

5.   awful _____

6.   big _____

7.   new _____

8.   hard _____

9.   unusual _____

10.   friendly _____

11.   average _____

12.   start _____

k *Give directions—tell how to get from one location to the other. Write your directions on a separate piece of paper.*

Examples:

drug store → Farmer's Market *Go one and a half blocks to Dixon Avenue, turn left and go up two blocks. You'll see it around the corner on Hill Street.*

Plaza Theater → Circus Disco *Go down Oak Street two blocks to Central Avenue, turn right and go to the end of the street. You'll see it on the left side.*

1. Book City → Grady's Hardware
2. Holiday Hotel → Marino Restaurant
3. Fifi's Beauty Salon → National Bank
4. Sunset Park → Wong's Kitchen
5. gas station → public library
6. Rose Cafe → Gold's Department Store

l *Make original sentences using the following prepositions.*

Example: on _They live on Bond Street._

1. of _____

2. for _____

3. from _____

4. in _____

5. at _____

6. to _____

7. with _____

m *Circle the letter next to the most appropriate response.*

1. When's Sam coming home?

   A. By bus.
   B. In an hour.
   C. A little while ago.
   D. To rest.

2. What kind of weather do you like?

   A. Sunny and warm.
   B. Big and strong.
   C. Slow and easy.
   D. Polite and friendly.

3. Which hat do you want?

   A. It's not expensive.
   B. I like cowboy hats.
   C. It's the right size.
   D. I'll take the red one.

4. How often do they have picnics?

   A. At the park.
   B. This Sunday.
   C. Once or twice a month.
   D. They're having one today.

5. Where have you been?

   A. On time.
   B. At the movies.
   C. In a hurry.
   D. Very busy.

6. What do you say when you're late?

   A. I'm glad.
   B. I'm sorry.
   C. I give up.
   D. It isn't worth it.

7. Why do some people work so hard?

   A. They have good jobs.
   B. They're unemployed.
   C. They want to make a lot of money.
   D. They want to have more free time.

8. Why is Joe always tired?

   A. He eats too much.
   B. He never does any work.
   C. He has a lot of friends.
   D. He doesn't get enough sleep.

9. How do you like your coffee?

   A. With cream and sugar.
   B. In the morning.
   C. For breakfast.
   D. From Brazil.

10. What did you do yesterday afternoon?

    A. I was with some friends.
    B. I was happy.
    C. I played basketball.
    D. I got very tired.

CHAPTER ELEVEN

Infinitive
of purpose
Present perfect
with ''just''

Present perfect
with ''already''
and ''yet''

a *What have they just done?*

1. They've just seen a movie.

2. He's just won a game of chess.

3. _____

4. _____

5. he has justdy booght a news paper

6. _____

7. _____

8. _____

PAST SIMPLE

He She I You We They	took a shower received a telegram called the hospital	a few minutes ago.

PRESENT PERFECT with JUST

He She	's (has)		taken a shower.
I You We They	've (have)	just	received a telegram. called the hospital.

b *Make sentences using the present perfect with **just**.*

Examples: Sam closed his shop five minutes ago.

He's just closed his shop.

I visited my uncle this afternoon.

I've just visited my uncle.

1. Peter washed the car a little while ago.

   _____

2. Jimmy and Linda came home a few minutes ago.

   _____

3. Mr. and Mrs. Golo moved into their new apartment this week.

   _____

4. They bought a television yesterday.

   _____

5. Mr. Bascomb read the newspaper a couple of minutes ago.

   _____

6. We saw that movie last night.

   _____

7. Mabel wrote a letter to her sister this morning.

   _____

8. I called the office a few seconds ago.

   _____

9. My brother found a job the day before yesterday.

   _____

She's going to the post office.

She's going to	get a package. buy some stamps. send some letters.

She's going to the post office to	get a package. buy some stamps. send some letters.

c *Combine the following sentences as indicated.*

Examples:

Sam is going outside. He's going to work in the garden.

Sam is going outside to work in the garden.

Otis and Gloria have gone to the museum. They want to see the new exhibition.

Otis and Gloria have gone to the museum to see the new exhibition.

1. Mabel has gone to the market. She wants to get some milk.

   _____

2. Barbara and Tino are going to the park. They're going to play tennis.

   _____

3. Barney has gone to the garage. He wants to talk to Nick.

   _____

4. Maria has gone home. She's going to take a shower.

   _____

5. We're going to the post office. We're going to send some letters.

   _____

6. Fred has gone to the bank. He wants to get a loan.

   _____

7. Mrs. Golo has gone to the kitchen. She's going to make some coffee.

   _____

8. I'm going downtown. I want to see a movie.

   _____

9. Jimmy and Linda are going to the store. They want to buy some candles.

   _____

PRESENT PERFECT with ALREADY   Affirmative

He She	's (has)			
I You We They	've (have)	already	seen visited been to	the museum.

d   *Answer the following questions using the present perfect with* **already**.

Examples: Is Mabel going to make dinner?

No, she's already made dinner.

Are Jimmy and Linda going to buy a dictionary?

No, they've already bought one.

1.   Is Dr. Pasto going to write a book about the South Pacific?

_____

2.   Is Nancy going to travel around the world?

_____

3.   Are Mr. and Mrs. Golo going to paint the bedroom?

_____

4.   Are they going to buy a television?

_____

5.   Is Peter going to wash the car?

_____

6.   Is Maria going to read the newspaper?

_____

7.   Are the Browns going to have dinner?

_____

8.   Is Tino going to call Barbara?

_____

9.   Are Jimmy and Linda going to do their homework?

_____

PRESENT PERFECT with YET   Negative

He She	hasn't (has not)	seen		
I You We They	haven't (have not)	visited been to	the museum	yet.

e   *Make negative sentences using the present perfect with yet.*

Examples: Mr. Golo has already repaired the stove. (the refrigerator)

But he hasn't repaired the refrigerator yet.

Our friends have already met Mayor Connors. (his wife)

But they haven't met his wife yet.

1.   Mabel has already written to her sister. (her brother)

_____

2.   Jimmy has already washed the dishes. (the glasses)

_____

3.   They've already cleaned the kitchen. (the living room)

_____

4.   Mr. Bascomb has already given money to the City Hospital. (the Wickam Library)

_____

5.   Maria has already called Peter's office. (his house)

_____

6.   Mr. and Mrs. Golo have already visited Mexico. (Brazil)

_____

7.   They've already eaten Mexican food. (Brazilian food)

_____

8.   Nancy has already gone out with Barney. (Nick)

_____

9.   I've already been to the bank. (the post office)

_____

112

f *Make original sentences using the present perfect with the following words.*

Examples: yet *I haven't read the newspaper yet.*
twice *She's been to the library twice this week.*
ever *Have you ever ridden a motorcycle?*

1. for _____

2. since _____

3. already _____

4. yet _____

5. just _____

6. ever _____

7. never _____

8. three times _____

9. recently _____

g *Complete the following sentences.*

Example: She's happy because *she got the job.*

1. They've just _____

2. Have you ever _____

3. I'm sorry _____

4. Most of my friends _____

5. Are you sure _____

6. We've decided _____

7. She's too busy _____

8. Do they have enough money _____

9. On my way home, I _____

10. You'll be happy to know that _____

h *Nancy is sending Peter a note inviting him to a picnic. Rewrite Nancy's note. Put in the missing punctuation and capital letters.*

peter

we're having a picnic this saturday at city park would you like to come the picnic starts at 1 pm we're having hot dogs and hamburgers for lunch if you come please bring some drinks after lunch we're going to have a volleyball game

please call me and let me know if you're coming my number is 436-8527 i'm usually home in the evening

see you

nancy

_____

_____

_____

_____

_____

_____

_____

_____

_____

i *Write a short note inviting someone to a party. Describe what kind of party it is. Will there be food and entertainment? Indicate when and where the party will take place.*

_____

_____

_____

_____

_____

_____

_____

_____

j *Answer the following questions about yourself.*

1. When was the last time you went to a movie?

   _____

2. What's your idea of a good time?

   _____

3. What were you doing last night at seven o'clock?

   _____

4. Where is a good place to meet people?

   _____

5. How long have you studied English?

   _____

6. How often do you speak English outside of class?

   _____

7. What is one thing you would like to do better?

   _____

8. What kind of food do you like?

   _____

9. Why do so many people eat junk food?

   _____

10. How are men different from women? (Give one example.)

    _____

11. Do you think it's better to have a large family or a small family?

    _____

12. Do you think it's more important to have a lot of money or a lot of friends?

    _____

13. Where would you like to go on your next vacation?

    _____

b *Write sentences using the present perfect with* ***for*** *or* ***since***.

Examples: The last time Barney received a letter was three months ago.

He hasn't received a letter for three months.

The last time we went to the mountains was in January.

We haven't been to the mountains since January.

1. The last time Maria had a party was in December.

_____

2. The last time she saw a movie was three weeks ago.

_____

3. The last time I spoke to her was last weekend.

_____

4. The last time we watched television was last Saturday.

_____

5. The last time Barbara and Tino played tennis was two weeks ago.

_____

6. The last time they went to the beach was in October.

_____

7. The last time Barney shaved was a few days ago.

_____

8. The last time he called Nancy was last week.

_____

9. The last time she fed the cat was on Tuesday.

_____

10. The last time Marty had an ice cream cone was two days ago.

_____

120

c   *Complete the following sentences using the most appropriate expressions from the list below. Use each expression only once.*

out of shape	right away	So far
I don't mind.	number one	get out of here
It's for the birds.	It's too bad	It isn't worth it.
So long.	I'm broke.	old fashioned
make sure	in a bad mood	

Examples: City Bank is the _number one_ bank in town.
(best)

I can't recommend Joe's Cafe. *It's for the birds.*
(It's no good.)

1. This has been a good year. _____ , everything has gone well.
(up to now)

2. I'm taking this package to Barbara and Tino. I want to _____ they get it.
(be certain)

3. They're a young couple, but they have a lot of _____ ideas.
(traditional)

4. You can turn on the radio. _____
(It's OK with me.)

5. Don't talk to Johnnie now. He's _____ .
(upset)

6. Please come _____ . I need your help.
(immediately)

7. I don't like this place. Let's _____ .
(leave)

8. _____ Albert can't play football with his friends.
(It's unfortunate)

9. He needs to get more exercise. He's _____ .
(in poor physical condition)

10. Don't try to repair that old typewriter. _____
(It's too much trouble.)

11. Can you loan me ten dollars? _____
(I don't have any money.)

12. I have to go now. _____
(Good-bye.)

d   *Write a short dialogue using at least three expressions from the list in Exercise c, above.*

e *Insert a or the if necessary.*

(1) Last night Peter and Maria had _____ dinner in _____ small Italian restaurant. (2) They both love _____ Italian food. (3) Maria ordered _____ plate of spaghetti with _____ tomato sauce. (4) Peter ordered _____ lasagna and _____ bottle of wine. (5) _____ spaghetti and _____ lasagna were very good, but _____ wine was _____ little too sweet. (6) Peter called _____ waiter and he brought them another bottle of wine. (7) This time, _____ wine was excellent. (8) For dessert, Maria had _____ piece of chocolate cake and Peter had _____ strawberries and _____ cream. (9) After _____ dessert, they each had _____ cup of espresso coffee. (10) They enjoyed their dinner very much, and Peter gave _____ waiter _____ big tip. (11) _____ waiter smiled and waved at Peter and Maria as they walked out of _____ restaurant.

f *Write original sentences using the following words.*

Example: quickly *Time passes quickly when you're having fun.* _____

1. better _____

2. change _____

3. next _____

4. while _____

5. afternoon _____

6. distance _____

7. although _____

8. nothing _____

9. spend _____

10. far _____

11. alone _____

12. several _____

g *Complete the following sentences using the most appropriate phrasal verbs from the list below. Use each phrasal verb only once.*

take back	go over	look up to	pay back
turn down	fill in	get through	put off
go away	turn up	pull up	
stand up for	run after	take off	

Examples: Please *go away*_____ . I want to be alone.
         (leave)

Look! The cat *is running after* the dog.
            (is chasing)

1. You must _____ this form before you see the doctor.
   (complete)

2. If it's too hot in here, you can _____ your coat.
   (remove)

3. Ed loves to eat. He never _____ a free meal.
   (refuses)

4. I'm trying to _____ my homework so I can watch TV.
   (finish)

5. When are you going to _____ the money you borrowed?
   (repay)

6. Peter is at the office. He _____ some reports.
   (is studying)

7. I'm busy this week. Let's _____ our meeting until next Monday.
   (postpone)

8. Please go to the library and _____ those books.
   (return)

9. What's wrong with Fred? He always _____ late.
   (arrives)

10. You have to _____ your friends when they're in trouble.
    (defend)

11. I _____ my father. He's an intelligent man.
    (respect)

12. We called a cab, and ten minutes later a taxi _____ in front of our house.
    (stopped)

h *Write a short dialogue using at least three phrasal verbs from the list in Exercise g, above.*

i   *Paradise Island and Storm Island are both small resort islands in the South Pacific. Write a short composition about these two islands, comparing the weather, entertainment, food, service, and prices.*

124

j *Add question tags to the following sentences.*

Examples: They've gone home. *They've gone home, haven't they?*

They won't come back. *They won't come back, will they?*

1. Mr. Bascomb is very busy. _____

2. He doesn't have much free time. _____

3. He has a lot of responsibility. _____

4. You've met him. _____

5. You were at his office. _____

6. You went there for a job interview. _____

7. You'd like to work for Mr. Bascomb. _____

8. He didn't give you a job. _____

9. You haven't found anything yet. _____

10. You won't give up. _____

k *The following sentences have mistakes in grammar. Find the mistakes and rewrite the sentences correctly.*

Examples: He's ~~very~~ tired to play tennis. *He's too tired to play tennis.*

He ~~hasn't slept~~ last night. *He didn't sleep last night.*

1. It's two weeks that she's here. _____

2. She called me three times since Sunday. _____

3. I have seen a boring movie yesterday. _____

4. I was sleeping when the movie was ending. _____

5. Look! A cat chases a dog! _____

6. You aren't seeing that every day. _____

7. A dog is usually more smart than a cat. _____

8. Cats don't have no brains. _____

9. Why you don't like cats? _____

10. Cats are the friendly animals. _____

13

CHAPTER THIRTEEN

Superlative   Go + -ing form

a *Write a sentence for each picture using the superlative form.*

1. The Mona Lisa/valuable painting

   The Mona Lisa is the most valuable painting in the world.

2. The Sears Tower/tall building

   The Sears Tower is the tallest building in the world.

3. Lake Superior/big lake

   _____

   _____

4. Mount Everest/high mountain

   _____

   _____

5. The Nile/long river

   _____

   _____

6. Shakespeare/popular author

   _____

   _____

7. English/important language

   _____

   _____

8. Vatican City/small independent state

   _____

SHORT-WORD COMPARATIVE + SUPERLATIVE

old strong	older stronger	oldest strongest

big fat	bigger fatter	biggest fattest

pretty friendly	prettier friendlier	prettiest friendliest

Irregular

good bad	better worse	best worst

LONG-WORD COMPARATIVE + SUPERLATIVE

popular elegant	more popular more elegant	most popular most elegant

b   *Make questions using the superlative form.*

Examples:

All of those children are smart. *Which one is the smartest?*

All of those apples are big. *Which one is the biggest?*

All of those girls are pretty. *Which one is the prettiest?*

All of those watches are expensive. *Which one is the most expensive?*

1.   All of those boys are thin. _____

2.   All of those women are busy. _____

3.   All of those men are successful. _____

4.   All of those girls are athletic. _____

5.   All of those cameras are good. _____

6.   All of those cars are economical. _____

7.   All of those boxes are light. _____

8.   All of those jobs are difficult. _____

9.   All of those clocks are old. _____

10.   All of those packages are heavy. _____

11.   All of those knives are sharp. _____

12.   All of those chairs are comfortable. _____

c   *Today is Thursday. What are they doing this weekend?*

1. *They're going camping.*

2. *He's going horseback riding.*

3.

4.

5.

6.

7.

8.

d *Complete the following sentences using because, but, so, and although.*

Examples: He can't speak Spanish, _although_ he lived in Mexico for five years.

Yesterday the weather was terrible, _but_ today it's beautiful.

She needed some money, _so_ she went to the bank.

1. The party wasn't very good, _____ we left early.

2. They like to dance _____ it's fun.

3. His apartment is small, _____ he likes it.

4. I don't have a car, _____ I walk to work.

5. She's taking her umbrella, _____ it isn't raining.

6. I'm making a sandwich _____ I'm hungry.

7. I was sick last night, _____ I feel fine now.

8. _____ she studies very hard, she doesn't get good grades.

9. She went to bed early _____ she was tired.

e *Complete the following sentences using suitable prepositions.*

Example: You can't see the dog because it's _behind_ the tree.

1. Fido usually enters the house _____ the back door.

2. I feel sorry _____ him because he doesn't sleep well _____ night.

3. My sister is getting married _____ a man _____ South America.

4. They're going to have their wedding _____ the end _____ this month.

5. They plan to live _____ a farm _____ Argentina.

6. Mr. Barnes will retire _____ his job _____ a few years.

7. He wants to take a trip _____ the world.

8. I'm writing a letter _____ a friend _____ mine _____ Japan.

9. She stayed _____ my family _____ a couple _____ weeks last year.

f *Sandy Benton is applying for a job at the Sunshine Travel Company. Look over her application for employment.*

APPLICATION FOR EMPLOYMENT

Name _Sandra Benton_   Position of _Tour Manager_

Address _1835 Sunset Avenue_   Salary Range _$900-$1,100/month_

City/State/Zip _Wickam City, Calif. 96210_   Telephone _643-7710_

PREVIOUS EMPLOYMENT (last job first)

1. Name of Company _Grand Hotel_

     Address of Company _794 Main Street Wickam City, California 96210_

     Dates of Employment (from) _6/87_ (to) _present_ Position _Receptionist_

     Reason for Leaving _I want to see the world._

2. Name of Company _Magnolia Restaurant_

     Address of Company _2050 Beacon Street Wickam City, California 96210_

     Dates of Employment (from) _2/85_ (to) _5/87_ Position _Waitress_

     Reasons for Leaving _I got tired of being a waitress._

REFERENCES

     Name   Address

1. _Roger Mason 936 Lime Street Wickam City, California 96210_
2. _Alma Sparks 4361 Bronson Avenue Springfield, California 97400_

EDUCATION

University or College _Wickam State University_

Number of years _4 years_   Degree(s) _Bachelor's Degree in Spanish_

High School _Riverside High School_ Did you graduate? _yes_

GENERAL INFORMATION (hobbies, sports, special interests, etc.)

My hobbies are collecting stamps and playing the guitar. I enjoy sports, especially tennis and skiing. And I love to travel.

Date _____ Signature _Sandra Benton_

g *Complete this application for employment. You can apply for any job you want.*

APPLICATION FOR EMPLOYMENT

Name _____ Position of _____

Address _____ Salary Range _____

City/State/Zip _____ Telephone _____

PREVIOUS EMPLOYMENT (last job first)

1. Name of Company _____

   Address of Company _____

   Dates of Employment (from) _____ (to) _____ Position _____

   Reason for Leaving _____

2. Name of Company _____

   Address of Company _____

   Dates of Employment (from) _____ (to) _____ Position _____

   Reasons for Leaving _____

REFERENCES

      Name   Address

1. _____

2. _____

EDUCATION

University or College _____

Number of years _____ Degree(s) _____

High School _____ Did you graduate? _____

GENERAL INFORMATION (hobbies, sports, special interests, etc.)

_____

_____

Date _____ Signature _____

Sandy Benton is having a job interview with Mr. Winkle, president of Sunshine Travel.

MR. WINKLE:	Good morning, Miss Benton.
MISS BENTON:	Good morning.
MR. WINKLE:	So you want to be a tour manager.
MISS BENTON:	That's right.
MR. WINKLE:	Have you ever worked in the travel business?
MISS BENTON:	No, but I've traveled to a lot of foreign countries. And I can speak three languages.
MR. WINKLE:	That's good. What kind of work experience do you have?
MISS BENTON:	Right now I'm working at the Wickham Hotel as a recepionist. Before that, I was a waitress at the Magnolia Restaurant.
MR. WINKLE:	Tell me more about yourself, Miss Benton. What are your strong points?
MISS BENTON:	Well, I'm friendly. I like people. And I'm a hard worker.
MR. WINKLE:	Why do you want to work for this company?
MISS BENTON:	Sunshine Travel has a very good reputation. You're the best travel agency in town.
MR. WINKLE:	Thank you. Do you have any questions, Miss Benton?
MISS BENTON:	Yes, how much is the starting salary?
MR. WINKLE:	A thousand dollars a month, plus living expenses.
MISS BENTON:	That sounds good.
MR. WINKLE:	Yes, it's a good job. I'll look over your application and call you in a few days.
MISS BENTON:	Thank you.

h *Answer the following questions about the interview.*

1. What job is Miss Benton applying for? _____

2. Has she ever worked in the travel business? _____

3. Where is she working now? _____

4. What are Miss Benton's strong points? _____

_____

5. Why does she want to work for Sunshine Travel? _____

_____

6. How much is the starting salary? _____

7. Do you think she'll get the job? Why? _____

_____

i *You're at a job interview. You can apply for any job you want. Complete the following sentences with information about yourself. Use the interview on page 133 as a model.*

EMPLOYER: Good morning, _____ .

YOU: _____ .

EMPLOYER: Please sit down.

YOU: _____ .

EMPLOYER: So you want to be a _____ .

YOU: _____ .

EMPLOYER: Where are you working now?

YOU: _____ .

EMPLOYER: How many different jobs have you had?

YOU: _____ .

EMPLOYER: How long have you lived in this city?

YOU: _____ .

EMPLOYER: Tell me more about yourself. What are your strong points?

YOU: _____ .

EMPLOYER: How's your health?

YOU: _____ .

EMPLOYER: Why do you want to work for this company?

YOU: _____ .

EMPLOYER: How much do you expect to earn?

YOU: _____ .

EMPLOYER: How did you find out about this job?

YOU: _____ .

EMPLOYER: I'll look over your application and call you in a few days.

YOU: _____ .

CHAPTER FOURTEEN

Used to

Verb + object + infinitive

Adjective + infinitive

Who/that/which

THEN NOW

a Mr. Fleetwood used to work as a salesman for the Star Insurance Company. Now he is president of the company. His lifestyle has changed a lot since he became president. *Write sentences about Mr. Fleetwood with used to.*

1. be a salesman/president of the company

He used to be a salesman, but now he's president of the company.

2. live in a small apartment/big house

_____

_____

_____

3. drive an old car/a big new car

_____

_____

_____

4. eat at Joe's Cafe/Maxime's

_____

_____

_____

5. buy his clothes at the Wickam Department Store/ Continental Men's Shop

_____

_____

_____

Affirmative

He She I You We They	used to	watch television every day. play basketball after school. take the bus in the morning.

b   *Write sentences with **used to** and **anymore**.*

Examples: They/dance at the Disco Club

They used to dance at the Disco Club, but they don't anymore.

She/like rock music

She used to like rock music, but she doesn't anymore.

1.   He/listen to the radio

   _____

2.   I/take the bus to work

   _____

3.   She/work very hard

   _____

4.   We/travel a lot

   _____

5.   You/be late for everything

   _____

6.   He/smoke Cuban cigars

   _____

7.   She/wear short dresses

   _____

8.   They/live near the post office

   _____

9.   I/get up early

   _____

c   *Complete the following sentences.*

Examples: It's nice *to have a cup of coffee in the morning.*
It's crazy *to wear heavy clothes on a hot day.*
It's economical *to take the bus to work.*

1. It's smart _____

2. It's wonderful _____

3. It's difficult _____

4. It's unusual _____

5. It's important _____

6. It's crazy _____

7. It's fun _____

8. It's interesting _____

9. It's easy _____

d   *Complete the following sentences using suitable prepositions.*

Example: Sandy left ____*on*____ Friday and we haven't seen her *since* .

1. Jack has been a member _____ the Lions Club _____ many years.

2. He's lived _____ the same street _____ 1965.

3. My friends are returning _____ Mexico City _____ Saturday.

4. They're going to stay _____ us _____ a week.

5. Sam took Mabel _____ a nice restaurant _____ her birthday.

6. They've already spoken _____ your sister _____ the job _____ the post office.

7. She came home _____ the market _____ a lot of food.

8. The president is staying _____ the Ritz Hotel _____ Paris.

9. It usually doesn't rain much _____ the summer months.

DEFINING RELATIVE CLAUSES   Things As Subject

She picked up the cards It was my umbrella Here's the telegram	that/which	were on the floor. was in the car. arrived this morning.

e   *Combine the following sentences using the relative pronoun that.*

Examples: He picked up the phone. It was next to his bed.

He picked up the phone that was next to his bed.

She answered the letters. They arrived last week.

She answered the letters that arrived last week.

1. We took the typewriter. It was in the office.

_____

2. I saw the photographs. They were on the wall.

_____

3. She put away the magazines. They were in the living room.

_____

4. He ate the oranges. They were in the refrigerator.

_____

5. They drank the coffee. It was on the stove.

_____

6. I read the newspaper. It was on the table.

_____

7. He wanted the camera. It belonged to his father.

_____

8. She bought the shoes. They were on sale.

_____

9. They spent the money. It was in the bank.

_____

DEFINING RELATIVE CLAUSES People As Object (Contact Clauses)

The man		I used to know worked in a circus.
The people	(who/that)	you met last night are good friends of mine.
That's the girl		we saw at the park yesterday.

Things As Object (Contact Clauses)

The dress		she bought was on sale.
The paintings	(that/which)	we saw were very interesting.
That's the movie		Jimmy was talking about.

f *Combine the following sentences, as indicated.*

Examples: They did the work. It was easy.

The work they did was easy.

I saw the boy. He had a green coat.

The boy I saw had a green coat.

1. We went to the party. It was lots of fun.

_____

2. I talked to the girl. She has a nice personality.

_____

3. She made the coffee. It was delicious.

_____

4. We knew the man. He had a lot of ambition.

_____

5. He married the woman. She had a lot of money.

_____

6. They bought the house. It was very expensive.

_____

7. I went to the meeting. It was boring.

_____

8. We read the letter. It had some mistakes in it.

_____

g *Each of the following sentences has one mistake. Find the mistake in each sentence and rewrite the sentence correctly.*

Examples: I admire people which work hard.

I admire people who work hard.

She wore the dress it belonged to her mother.

She wore the dress that belonged to her mother.

The test was easy that we took last week.

The test that we took last week was easy.

1. They talked to the policeman he was standing on the corner.

_____

2. The meeting where I went to was boring.

_____

3. Did you see the girl which ran across the street?

_____

4. The cookies were delicious that your mother made.

_____

5. I'm looking for the magazines there were on the table.

_____

6. Do you know the people who lives across the street?

_____

7. The man lives next door is a doctor.

_____

8. Here are the magazines you asked for them.

_____

9. The movie was very interesting that we saw yesterday.

_____

10. The woman has a motorcycle who lives in apartment five.

_____

144

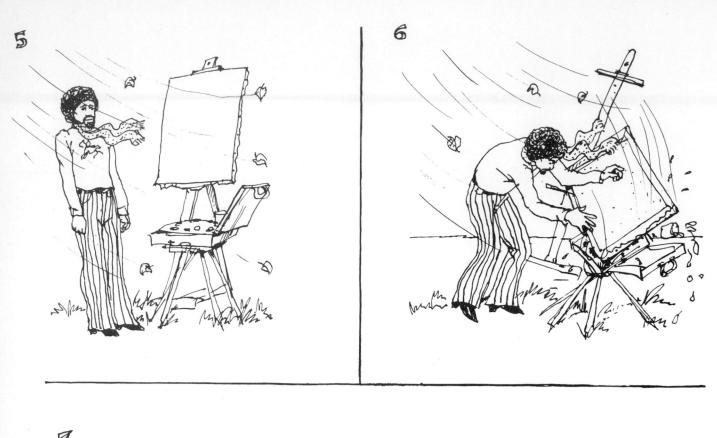

h *Write a short composition about Otis and his "masterpiece."*

park	painting	think	make
art equipment	beautiful	know	see
paints	masterpiece	paint	like
wind	man	start	want
canvas	woman	blow	buy
		fall	

CHAPTER FIFTEEN

The same as

As + adjective + as

As + adverb + as

Comparison of adverbs

Could/should

COMPARISON OF ADVERBS

	well.			
She works	hard.	She works	better	than the average person.
	carefully.		harder	
			more carefully	

a *Look at the pictures and make comparisons, as indicated.*

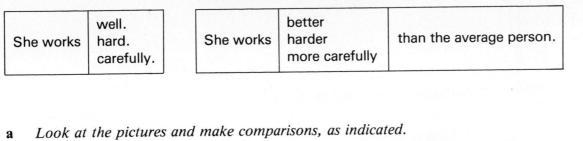

1. Mr. Bascomb speaks loudly.

   He speaks louder than Barbara.

Mr. Bascomb   **Barbara**

2. Susie listens carefully.

   _____

Susie   Marty

3. Fred sings badly.

   _____

Barney   **Fred**

4. Otis and Gloria dance well.

   _____

Otis and Gloria

Johnnie and Anne

148

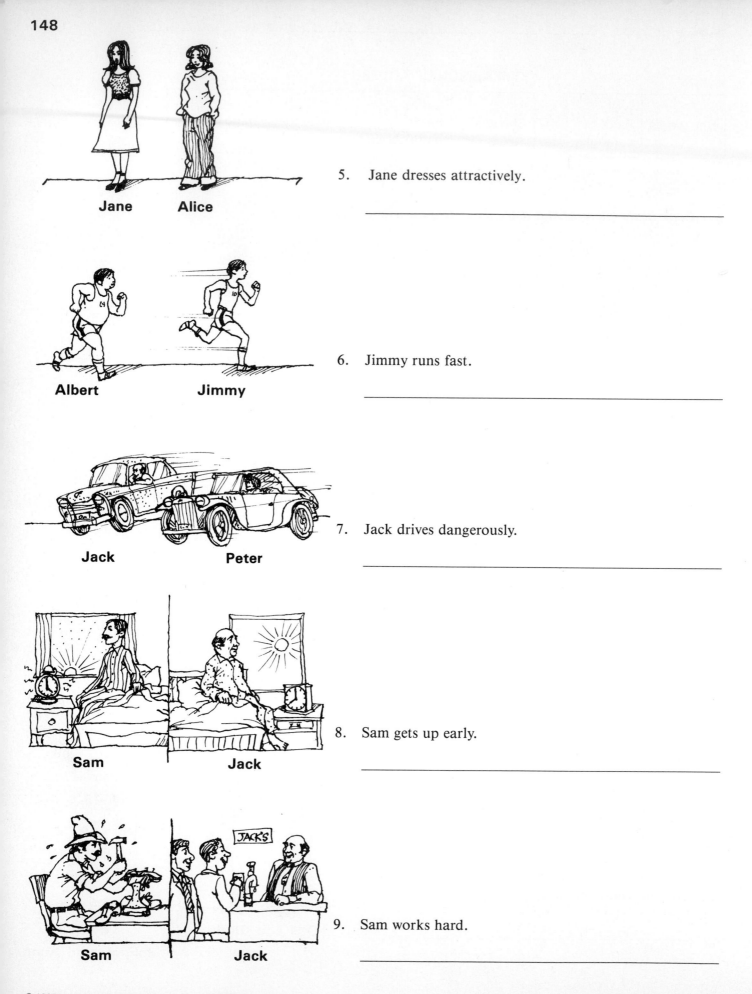

Jane   **Alice**

5. Jane dresses attractively.

_____

Albert   **Jimmy**

6. Jimmy runs fast.

_____

Jack   **Peter**

7. Jack drives dangerously.

_____

Sam   **Jack**

8. Sam gets up early.

_____

Sam   **Jack**

9. Sam works hard.

_____

She works	better harder more carefully	than	he does.

He doesn't work	as	well hard carefully	as	she does.

b   *Change the following sentences as indicated.*

Examples: Mr. Bascomb speaks louder than Barbara.

Barbara doesn't speak as loudly as Mr. Bascomb.

Susie listens more carefully than Marty.

Marty doesn't listen as carefully as Susie.

Fred sings worse than Barney.

Barney doesn't sing as badly as Fred.

1.   Linda studies harder than Albert.

_____

2.   Barbara works more carefully than Anne.

_____

3.   Peter drives faster than Tino.

_____

4.   Sam gives his time more generously than Mr. Bascomb.

_____

5.   Barney gets up earlier than Fred.

_____

6.   The Bascombs live more comfortably than the Browns.

_____

7.   Johnnie dances worse than Anne.

_____

8.   Barbara plays tennis better than Tino.

_____

9.   Jack drives more dangerously than Peter.

_____

MUCH

| He doesn't have as much work as she does. |

LESS

| He has less work than she does. |

MANY

| We don't have as many problems as they do. |

FEWER

| We have fewer problems than they do. |

c   *Make sentences using **fewer** and **less**.*

Examples: Mr. Golo doesn't read as much as his wife.

Mr. Golo reads less than his wife.

He doesn't have as many interests as she does.

He has fewer interests than she does.

1.   Albert doesn't have as much energy as Linda.

_____

2.   He doesn't exercise as much as she does.

_____

3.   Barbara doesn't have as many friends as Tino.

_____

4.   She doesn't meet as many people as he does.

_____

5.   We don't watch as much television as our neighbors.

_____

6.   They don't have as many interests as we do.

_____

7.   Barney doesn't travel as much as Nancy.

_____

8.   He doesn't have as much fun as she does.

_____

9.   I don't receive as many letters as you do.

_____

d *Look at the pictures and write a sentence for each one using* **could**.

1. Nancy/15 *Nancy could sail a boat when she was fifteen.*

2. Albert/8 _____

3. Anne/12 _____

4. Barbara/14 _____

5. Tino/9 _____

6. Tino/10 _____

7. Nancy/5 _____

8. Otis/7 _____

Negative

I He We	couldn't (could not)	go to the park have a picnic play tennis	yesterday because it was raining.

e *Change the following sentences as indicated.*

Examples: Anne wanted to sleep late, but she had to go to work.

Anne couldn't sleep late because she had to go to work.

She wanted to talk to Mr. Bascomb, but he was busy.

She couldn't talk to Mr. Bascomb because he was busy.

1. Jimmy wanted to play football, but he had to do his homework.

_____

2. Linda wanted to watch television, but she had to clean the kitchen.

_____

3. They wanted to buy a new radio, but they didn't have enough money.

_____

4. I wanted to pick up my package, but the post office was closed.

_____

5. Sam wanted to work in the garden, but it was too hot.

_____

6. Mabel wanted to make spaghetti, but she didn't have any tomatoes.

_____

7. They wanted to move the piano, but it was too heavy.

_____

8. Barbara wanted to wear her red dress, but it wasn't clean.

_____

9. We wanted to go to your party last week, but we were out of town.

_____

10. We wanted to call you, but we didn't have your telephone number.

_____

NAME _____ DATE _____

f *Look at the pictures and write a sentence for each one using **should**.*

1. *Marty should get to class on time.*

Marty

2. _____

Anne

3. _____

Jack

4. _____

Mrs. Golo

5. _____

Linda

6. _____

Mr. Bascomb

7. _____

Jack

8. _____

Jimmy

154

Negative

| She
We
They | shouldn't
(should not) | drive so fast.
spend so much money.
forget so easily. |

g *Make sentences using shouldn't.*

Examples: Peter drives fast, doesn't he?

Yes, he shouldn't drive so fast.

He spends a lot of money, doesn't he?

Yes, he shouldn't spend so much money.

He makes a lot of promises, doesn't he?

Yes, he shouldn't make so many promises.

1. Nancy hurries a lot, doesn't she?

_____

2. She drinks a lot of coffee, doesn't she?

_____

3. Your friends work hard, don't they?

_____

4. Marty eats a lot of ice cream, doesn't he?

_____

5. Mr. Golo misses a lot of meetings, doesn't he?

_____

6. He forgets easily, doesn't he?

_____

7. His wife complains a lot, doesn't she?

_____

8. She talks loudly, doesn't she?

_____

9. They worry a lot, don't they?

_____

h *Ed is going to the Rainbow Employment Agency for a nine o'clock interview with Mrs. Stone. He wants to get a job as a security guard. It is very important for him to make a good impression at the interview. What advice can you give Ed? Write sentences using* **should** *or* **shouldn't**.

Examples: sunglasses *He should take off his sunglasses.*

OR *He shouldn't wear sunglasses.*

1. shower _____

2. haircut _____

3. tennis shoes _____

4. coat and tie _____

5. Brutus _____

6. chocolates _____

7. cigar _____

Can you think of any other advice to give Ed? Do you have any advice for Mrs. Stone? What about for the security guard?

8. _____

9. _____

10. _____

i *What do you think Ed and Mrs. Stone will say to each other during the interview? Write a short dialogue between Ed and Mrs. Stone. You may want to use some of the following vocabulary and expressions.*

Nice to meet you.	It isn't worth it.	Get out of here.
What's the matter?	No problem.	I'll do my best.
Don't be afraid.	Whatever you say.	Good luck.
Are you serious?	You're hopeless/perfect.	See you later.

kind of work	qualifications	salary
security guard	experience	hours
present occupation	references	uniform

Mrs. Stone   Come in. I'm Mrs. Stone.

Ed

16

CHAPTER SIXTEEN

Review

a   *Complete the following sentences about Charlie and Lucy.*

1. Charlie Garrison is having lunch *at Lucy's Cafe* .

2. He's talking to _____ . She's the _____ of the cafe.

3. Charlie goes there because _____ .

4. Lucy likes Charlie because _____ .

5. She wants _____ Saturday night.

6. Charlie likes Lucy, but _____ .

7. _____ is calling Charlie.

8. Charlie says _____ to Lucy and _____ the cafe.

9. Lucy doesn't say _____ . She's _____ because _____

_____ .

b *Complete the following sentences using* **can, can't, will, won't, must, shall, would, should, shouldn't, could,** *and* **couldn't.**

Examples: Jane is always tired. She _*should*_ get more sleep.

I _*can't*_ tell you the time because I don't have a watch.

1.   Mr. Blakey is a good musician. He _____ play several instruments.

2.   Linda can't lift that box. It _____ be too heavy.

3.   Do you think Sam _____ be home for dinner tonight?

4.   Albert is getting fat. He _____ eat so much.

5.   Nancy _____ ride a bicycle when she was only five years old.

6.   Someone is at the door. _____ I see who it is?

7.   Susie is short. She _____ reach the glasses on the top shelf.

8.   Fred never misses a football game. He _____ like football.

9.   You look thirsty. _____ you like a cold drink?

10.   Jack drives dangerously. He _____ be more careful.

11.   It isn't raining anymore. You _____ need your umbrella.

12.   Maria _____ come to the party last night because she was sick.

13.   It's getting late. I hope we _____ have time to visit the Art Museum.

14.   Jimmy is a big boy now. You _____ worry about him.

15.   There isn't any food in the house. _____ we eat out tonight?

16.   Otis was a good athlete in high school. He _____ play every sport.

17.   Nancy is a very good pilot. She _____ have a lot of experience.

18.   Sam has a big appetite. He _____ eat four hamburgers.

19.   Don't worry. Jimmy _____ forget to wash the dishes.

20.   Mr. Poole worked hard but he _____ save any money last year.

RELATIVE CLAUSES   People As Object

The man The people That's the girl	(who/that)	I used to know worked in a circus. you met last night are good friends of mine. we saw at the park yesterday.

Things As Object

The dress The paintings That's the movie	(that/which)	she bought was on sale. we saw were very interesting. Jimmy was talking about.

c   *Change the following sentences as indicated.*

Examples: He's dancing with a woman who is taller than he is.

The woman he's dancing with is taller than he is.

She tells stories that are very interesting.

The stories she tells are very interesting.

1. She goes out with a boy who loves classical music.

   _____

2. They live in a city that has two airports.

   _____

3. I work for a man who is very generous.

   _____

4. He's looking at a magazine that has some beautiful photographs.

   _____

5. We're writing to a woman who lives in Panama.

   _____

6. She wears clothes that are very expensive.

   _____

7. You're talking to a man who is an expert on football.

   _____

8. He drives a car that is very economical.

   _____

162

d *Complete the following sentences using **who** or **that**.*

Examples: She works for a man *who is very generous*.

He drove a car *that made a lot of noise*.

1. I like people _____

2. We live in a town _____

3. We met someone _____

4. He lived in a house _____

5. I know a lady _____

6. She tells stories _____

7. She has a son _____

8. He's married to a woman _____

9. She bought a dress _____

10. Can you recommend a restaurant _____

e *Complete the following sentences.*

Example: Why don't they *go out more often?*

1. It's hard to _____

2. She feels sad because _____

3. Is it possible _____

4. You shouldn't _____

5. He's the most _____

6. It's too bad _____

7. How did _____

8. Do you mind if _____

9. The only problem is that _____

10. How do you feel when _____

11. The truth is _____

12. I hope _____

SHORT-WORD COMPARATIVE
+ SUPERLATIVE

old strong	older stronger	oldest strongest

LONG-WORD COMPARATIVE
+ SUPERLATIVE

original powerful	more original more powerful	most original most powerful

big fat	bigger fatter	biggest fattest

pretty friendly	prettier friendlier	prettiest friendliest

f *Fill in the missing words.*

Examples: small *smaller* *smallest*
happy *happier* *happiest*
successful *more successful* *most successful*

1. easy _____ _____

2. short _____ _____

3. interesting _____ _____

4. poor _____ _____

5. ugly _____ _____

6. serious _____ _____

7. hard _____ _____

8. athletic _____ _____

9. cheap _____ _____

10. lucky _____ _____

11. light _____ _____

12. fast _____ _____

13. comfortable _____ _____

14. friendly _____ _____

15. big _____ _____

g   *Complete the following sentences with a suitable adjective or adverb.*

Examples: I don't sing as (bad) ___*badly*___ as my sister.

She sings (loud) ___*louder*___ than you do.

My car is (practical) ___*more practical*___ than yours.

I'm the (busy) ___*busiest*___ person in my family.

1. Linda writes (good) _____ than Albert.

2. Barney talks (slow) _____ than most people.

3. Mr. Bascomb is (ambitious) _____ than Jack.

4. He works much (hard) _____ than the average person.

5. Nobody takes life as (serious) _____ as Mr. Bascomb.

6. Slim Skinner is the (thin) _____ boy in his class.

7. He doesn't learn as (quick) _____ as his sister.

8. Mrs. Hamby is (fat) _____ than her husband.

9. We live (economical) _____ than they do.

10. Dr. Pasto is the (sophisticated) _____ man in Wickam City.

11. Mrs. Golo is the (bad) _____ dancer I've ever seen.

12. Maria is (practical) _____ than Peter.

13. He doesn't plan as (careful) _____ as she does.

14. Nancy is the (adventurous) _____ woman I know.

15. Fred is the (lazy) _____ man in town.

16. Mr. Poole drives (bad) _____ than his wife.

17. You dress (fashionable) _____ than they do.

18. Your suitcase is (heavy) _____ than mine.

19. Gloria doesn't dance as (good) _____ as Otis.

20. He's the (good) _____ dancer around.

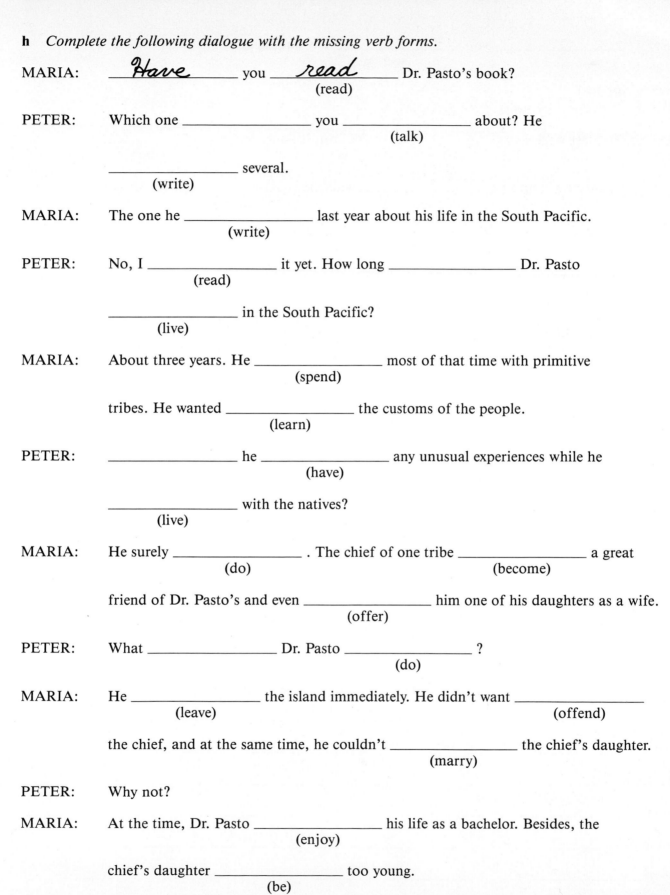

h *Complete the following dialogue with the missing verb forms.*

MARIA: ___*Have*___ you ___*read*___ Dr. Pasto's book?
(read)

PETER: Which one _____ you _____ about? He
(talk)

_____ several.
(write)

MARIA: The one he _____ last year about his life in the South Pacific.
(write)

PETER: No, I _____ it yet. How long _____ Dr. Pasto
(read)

_____ in the South Pacific?
(live)

MARIA: About three years. He _____ most of that time with primitive
(spend)

tribes. He wanted _____ the customs of the people.
(learn)

PETER: _____ he _____ any unusual experiences while he
(have)

_____ with the natives?
(live)

MARIA: He surely _____ . The chief of one tribe _____ a great
(do)   (become)

friend of Dr. Pasto's and even _____ him one of his daughters as a wife.
(offer)

PETER: What _____ Dr. Pasto _____ ?
(do)

MARIA: He _____ the island immediately. He didn't want _____
(leave)   (offend)

the chief, and at the same time, he couldn't _____ the chief's daughter.
(marry)

PETER: Why not?

MARIA: At the time, Dr. Pasto _____ his life as a bachelor. Besides, the
(enjoy)

chief's daughter _____ too young.
(be)

PETER: _____ you _____ any photographs of the places Dr.
(see)

Pasto _____ ?
(visit)

MARIA: Yes, last week I _____ to Dr. Pasto's house and he _____
(go)   (show)

me some pictures he _____ while he _____ in Africa
(take)   (travel)

last summer. Dr. Pasto _____ an excellent photographer, and the
(be)

pictures _____ very well.
(come out)

PETER: Hmm, someday I'd like _____ Dr. Pasto and _____
(visit)   (hear)

his stories. _____ you _____ if he _____
(know)   (work)

on any new books?

MARIA: Yes, he _____ just _____ a book _____
(start)   (call)

The Beautiful World of Butterflies.

PETER: _____ you _____ it _____ a success?
(think)   (be)

MARIA: Sure. Everyone _____ Dr. Pasto's books.
(read)

i   *Write original sentences using the following words.*

Example: recommend *Can you recommend a good doctor?*

1. best _____

2. promise _____

3. most _____

4. everything _____

5. same _____

6. worse _____

7. again _____

8. different from _____

1

2

3

4

j *Write a short composition about Dr. Philips, the university professor.*

mathematics	car	teach	know
class	flat tire	understand	use
university	jack	leave	repair
intelligent	trunk	drive	walk
respected	bum	have	come
students	easy	take	help